THE GREEN-FINGERED GARDENER

seasonal flower gardens

THE GREEN-FINGERED GARDENER

seasonal flower gardens

a practical guide to gardening
through the year

peter mchoy

southwater

This edition is published by Southwater

Southwater is an imprint of Anness Publishing Ltd
Hermes House, 88–89 Blackfriars Road, London SE1 8HA
tel. 020 7401 2077; fax 020 7633 9499
www.southwaterbooks.com; info@anness.com

© Anness Publishing Ltd 2000, 2003

This edition distributed in the UK by The Manning Partnership Ltd,
6 The Old Dairy, Melcombe Road, Bath BA2 3LR;
tel. 01225 478 444; fax 01225 478 440; sales@manning-partnership.co.uk

This edition distributed in the USA and Canada by National Book Network,
4720 Boston Way, Lanham, MD 20706;
tel. 301 459 3366; fax 301 459 1705; www.nbnbooks.com

This edition distributed in Australia by Pan Macmillan Australia,
Level 18, St Martins Tower, 31 Market St, Sydney, NSW 2000;
tel. 1300 135 113; fax 1300 135 103; customer.service@macmillan.com.au

This edition distributed in New Zealand by The Five Mile Press (NZ) Ltd,
PO Box 33–1071 Takapuna, Unit 11/101–111 Diana Drive, Glenfield, Auckland 10;
tel. (09) 444 4144; fax (09) 444 4518; fivemilenz@clear.net.nz

A CIP catalogue record for this book is available from the British Library.

Publisher: Joanna Lorenz
Senior Editor: Caroline Davison
Project Editor: Jeremy Smith
Production Controller: Karina Han
Designers: Mark Latter, Patrick Mcleavey & Jo Brewer
Photographer: Peter Anderson
Illustrator: Michael Shoebridge

Previously published as *The Seasonal Flower Garden*

1 3 5 7 9 10 8 6 4 2

■ **PAGE ONE**
A beautiful meandering
country path is framed by
a charming selection of
shrubs and perennials.

■ **PAGE TWO**
The flower garden in
summer, clothed in a riot
of greens, pinks, yellows
and reds.

■ **PAGE THREE**
An exciting mixture of
spicy colours makes this
border a stunning focal
point for the garden.

■ **ABOVE**
Waterlilies are among
the most beautiful of all
plants, lighting up a water
garden in summer.

■ **RIGHT**
The borders on each side
of this wide pathway have
been edged with a
selection of perennials.

CONTENTS

INTRODUCTION

ABOVE: *Spring is a good time to plant herbaceous plants ready for summer.*

Gardening is, above all, a practical hobby. You can, of course, simply admire gardens created by others, but anyone worthy of being called a gardener enjoys the challenges of growing plants. Success does not come without effort or know-how, however, even for the experienced gardener. For the beginner, success depends largely on sound advice for all those essential tasks that lie behind the well-kept garden that we all admire. This book has been designed to provide just that kind of down-to-earth practical help that we all need from time to time.

There is no substitute for being able to see how something is

ABOVE: *Adequate feeding is one of the keys to success for container plants.*

done. Not only are pictures clearer than any amount of written instructions, but they reassure you that the advice is based on actual experience. With a range of step-by-step illustrations, as well as plenty of inspirational pictures to spur you on, this book provides a dependable gardening companion that is always on hand to help: your own expert to show you how things are done, and when.

ABOVE: *As soon as the summer display is over, replant containers for a spring display.*

You will find this book invaluable not only because jobs are illustrated with step-by-step pictures, but also because they are arranged by season, too. If you are not sure what you should be doing now, this book will tell you *and* show you.

ABOVE: *Christmas roses are hardy, but protection will prevent mud splashes.*

The gardening season

Jobs have been arranged by seasons rather than precise weeks, as gardening is very much dependent on the weather, and precise dates can be misleading and even potentially hazardous to your plants.

You cannot garden successfully by the calendar alone. Frosts can come early in autumn or occur unexpectedly in early summer. The ground may be frozen when you would like to be planting, or too dry when you want to sow your summer seeds. Use the suggested timings as a guide, but be prepared to bring things forward or put them back to suit your own area and the particular season.

The most time-critical jobs are likely to be in spring and autumn, and when frost-tender plants are put outside or taken in. If in doubt about the best time, it is always worth making a note of when your local parks department does the job.

Winter jobs, on the other hand, are usually less time-critical and in many cases it will not matter if you move a job backwards or forwards by as much as a month. This is fortunate as it gives you the opportunity to delay a job if the weather is harsh, and to make up for lost time during those brighter spells.

LEFT: *Azaleas are popular shrubs, but they require an acid soil. You can use a simple kit to check the soil acidity.*

RIGHT: *Modern solidago hybrids are excellent border plants for late summer.*

LEFT: *Varieties of* Anemone x hybrida *and* A. hupehensis *come into their own when most border flowers are over.*

RIGHT: Sorbus aucuparia *will sometimes retain its berries into winter if birds don't eat them first.*

SPRING

*This is a time when gardeners need no encouragement.
With lengthening days, the air less chilly, and plump buds and birdsong
to stir the imagination, it is the time when gardeners cannot wait to start
propagating and planting. Early spring is a time for caution, however,
as winter seldom comes to a convenient end as spring approaches.
One of the most common causes of disappointment for novice gardeners is
sowing or planting too early – especially outdoors. Often, plants and
seeds put out several weeks later in the season overtake ones planted
earlier because they are less likely to receive a check to growth.*

OPPOSITE: *Even small spring flowers make a
strong display, like this group of narcissi,
pulmonarias, and* Anemone blanda.

ABOVE: *Tulips are among the most beautiful
spring flowers, but they look even better when
interplanted with forget-me-nots.*

EARLY SPRING

IN COLD REGIONS THE WEATHER CAN still be icy in early spring, but in mild climates you can make a start on many outdoor jobs. If sowing or planting outdoors, bear in mind that soil temperature as well as air temperature is important. Few seeds will germinate if the soil temperature is below 7°C (45°F), so use a soil thermometer to check before you sow.

JOBS IN BRIEF

The Flower Garden

- ❏ Finish planting shrubs
- ❏ Keep newly planted shrubs moist at the roots
- ❏ Plant container-grown shrubs
- ❏ Plant herbaceous plants
- ❏ Sow hardy annuals
- ❏ Plant gladioli and summer bulbs
- ❏ Start mowing the lawn, but cut high initially
- ❏ Buy seeds and bulbs
- ❏ Spring prune shrubs, if applicable
- ❏ Tidy up the rock garden, and apply fresh stone chippings
- ❏ Watch out for pests and apply insecticide or fungicide if necessary

The Greenhouse and Conservatory

- ❏ Start off begonia and gloxinia tubers
- ❏ Pot up pelargonium and fuchsia cuttings rooted earlier
- ❏ Prick out or pot up seedlings sown earlier
- ❏ Increase ventilation on warm days
- ❏ Check plants for signs of pests and diseases, which can multiply rapidly as the temperatures rise

TOP LEFT: *Pot up cuttings as soon as they begin to grow vigorously.*

TOP RIGHT: *If planting a border, lay the plants out first so that you can visualize the result.*

RIGHT: *Dig out deep-rooted perennials.*

PLANTS AT THEIR BEST

Bergenia (non-woody evergreen)
Camellia (shrub)
Chionodoxa (bulb)
Crocus (bulb)
Eranthis hyemalis (bulb)
Garrya elliptica (shrub)
Helleborus orientalis (herbaceous)
Hyacinthus (bulb)
Iris reticulata (bulb)
Magnolia stellata (shrub)
Mahonia (shrub)
Muscari armeniacum (bulb)
Primula × *polyantha*
(herbaceous)
Prunus cerasifera (tree)
Tulipa kaufmanniana (bulb)

ABOVE: *A* Tulipa kaufmanniana *variety.*

LEFT: Iris reticulata.

BELOW: *Chionodoxas and crocuses.*

SOW HARDY ANNUALS

Hardy annuals are among the easiest plants to grow – they are undemanding of soil and are simply sown where they are to grow. Provided you thin overcrowded seedlings and give them a sunny position, the results are almost always bright and pleasing.

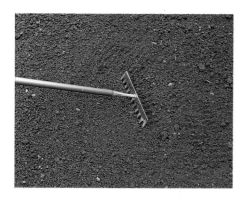

1 It pays to prepare the ground by clearing it of weeds, and raking the surface to a fine, crumbly structure.

2 If you are growing just for cutting, sow in rows in a spare piece of ground, but if you want to make a bright border of hardy annuals, 'draw' your design on the ground with sand and grit.

3 Use the corner of a hoe or rake to draw shallow drills, but change the direction of the drills from one block to the next to avoid a regimented appearance. Check the packet for spacing between rows.

4 Sprinkle the seeds as evenly as possible. If the weather is very dry, run water into the bottom of each drill first and allow it to soak in.

5 Write and insert a label, then cover the seeds by raking the soil back over the drills. Try not to disturb the seeds unnecessarily.

6 Water thoroughly if the soil is dry and rain is not forecast. Continue to water in dry weather until the seedlings have emerged.

SOWING BROADCAST

Sowing in rows makes thinning and weeding much easier – especially if you don't know what the seedlings look like and find it difficult to distinguish desirable seedlings from weeds. Sometimes, however, the seeds are sown broadcast (scattered randomly) to create a more informal patch of flowers. This is particularly useful for a packet of mixed annuals, for example, where you might want to create the appearance of a wild garden.

Scatter the seeds as evenly as possible (see above), then rake them in – first in one direction and then at right angles.

PLANT GLADIOLI

Gladioli are popular, and easy to grow, but their location in the flower garden needs careful thought. Grow them in rows in a spare piece of ground if you want them for cutting, but they look best planted in blocks or clusters when grown among companion plants.

OTHER BULBS TO PLANT

1 If you are growing gladioli for cutting rather than garden display, grow them in rows. Take out a trench as shown deep enough to cover the corms with about 8–10cm (3–4in) of soil. Deep planting reduces the need for staking.

2 Space the corms as recommended on the packet. Planting a double row like this makes supporting easier for tall varieties. Return the soil to the trench to cover them.

Most other summer-flowering bulbs, corms and tubers can be planted in the same way as gladioli, though it is too early to plant any very frost-sensitive plants as the shoots may emerge while frosts are still likely.

As a guide to planting depth, most bulbs should be covered with twice their own depth of soil. If the bulb is 3cm (1in) deep, cover it with 5cm (2in) of soil, though there are a few exceptions.

Some tubers tend to become very dry and shrivelled after a long period in storage. You can usually plump them up by soaking in water for a day before you plant, as with the anemone tubers shown.

3 If planting in a border among other plants, take out a roughly circular hole, place a group of about five or seven corms in the base, and return the soil. If the ground is heavy, dig in some sand or grit before planting the corms.

4 It is easy to forget where bulbs are planted in a border, so apart from labelling, insert a few small canes around them so that you don't accidentally hoe off the shoots before they emerge.

PLANT SHRUBS

Spring is an ideal time to plant shrubs. You can plant container-grown shrubs in any month provided the ground is not too frozen. However, spring is ideal because the soil is moist and also warm enough for new root growth to help the plant become established quickly.

1 Always clear the area of weeds, and dig out any deep-rooted perennials that will be difficult to eradicate if they grow within the root system of the shrub. Dig in plenty of garden compost or rotted manure.

2 Excavate a large hole, about twice the width of the pot or root-ball. To check the depth, place the plant in position and use a cane or stick across the hole to judge whether the shrub will be at its original depth in the soil.

3 If the roots are dry, water the plant thoroughly then leave for an hour. If roots are wound tightly around the inside of the pot, tease out some of the fine ones to encourage them to grow out into the soil.

4 Place the root-ball in the hole and check that the soil will be level with the potting soil in the root-ball. Return the soil, and firm it well to eliminate large air pockets.

5 To get your shrubs off to a good start, apply a general garden fertilizer at the recommended rate and sprinkle around the plant. Keep away from the stem. Water well.

6 'Balled' or 'root-wrapped' shrubs are sold with their roots wrapped in hessian (burlap) or a plastic material. Check the depth as before.

7 When the plant is in position, untie the wrapper and slide it out of the hole. Avoid disturbing the ball of soil around the roots.

8 Replace the soil, and firm well to eliminate large pockets of air. Apply fertilizer and water as described for container-grown plants.

9 It is worth mulching the ground after planting. It will conserve moisture and some mulches, such as chipped bark, look attractive too.

PLANT HERBACEOUS PLANTS

Herbaceous border plants can be planted at any time from containers, but most gardeners prefer to get them planted in spring so that they contribute to the summer show.

If you buy plants by mail order they may arrive as small root-wrapped plants, and these should be planted before the new shoots emerge, or are still very short.

1 If planting a border, lay the plants out first so that you can visualize the result (don't forget to allow for growth!). It is easier to move them around at this stage, before planting.

2 Water the plants about an hour before you start, and knock them out of their pots only when you are ready to plant.

ROOT-WRAPPED HERBACEOUS PLANTS

If your herbaceous plants are root-wrapped, keep them in a cool, shady place until you are ready to plant. Make sure that the plants are kept moist at all times.

Remove the wrapping only just before you are ready to plant. Spread the roots out widely within the planting hole before returning the soil.

Root-wrapped plants are more vulnerable than container-grown plants until they become established, so take extra care and keep them well watered.

3 Ensure the ground is clear of weeds before planting, and work methodically from the back of the border or from one end. Most can be planted with a trowel but you may need a spade for large plants.

4 Return the soil, making sure that the plant is at its original depth, and firm well to eliminate any large pockets of air that could cause the roots to dry out.

5 Water the plants thoroughly unless the weather is wet or heavy rain is forecast.

SPRING PRUNE SHRUBS

Only prune shrubs that you know require spring pruning, otherwise you may cut out the shoots that will bear this year's flowers. Advice is given below for some popular shrubs that need spring pruning, but if in doubt about others consult an encyclopedia that gives pruning information.

1 Prune shrubs grown for coloured winter stems shortly before new growth starts. These include *Cornus alba* and *Cornus stolonifera* varieties and *Salix alba* 'Chermesina' (syn. 'Britzensis'). Only prune plants that have been established for a few years.

2 Cut back all the stems to an outward-facing bud about 5cm (2in) from the ground or stump of old, hard wood.

3 Although the pruning seems drastic, new shoots will soon appear and by next winter will make a splendid sight. Prune annually if you feed and mulch the plants, otherwise every second spring.

4 Some popular grey-leaved shrubs, such as *Santolina chamaecyparissus* and *Helichrysum angustifolium*, need regular pruning if they are to remain neat and compact.

5 If you prune the plant regularly from a young age, prune back close to the base to a point where you can see new shoots developing. This may be as low as 10cm (4in) from the ground on some plants, but on old, woody plants you will have to leave a taller framework of woody shoots.

6 The plant will look bare and sparse after pruning, but within a month should be well clothed again.

7 *Buddleia davidii* produces its flowers at the tops of tall, lanky stems if left unpruned. Each spring, cut back all the shoots to within about two buds of the previous year's growth, close to the old stump.

8 Again, this type of pruning looks drastic but it will greatly enhance the look of the plant later in the year.

A few shrubs related to the blackberry are grown for their white winter stems. The shoots arise from ground level like raspberry canes, and these are best cut back every year. Cut all the stems off close to the ground. New shoots will soon grow and the plant will be just as attractive next winter.

PRUNE ROSES

Trials have shown that you can achieve very good results from hybrid tea (large-flowered) and floribunda (cluster-flowered) roses simply by cutting them roughly to an even height with secateurs (pruners) or a hedge trimmer, without worrying about the detailed pruning shown here. The conventional method is still practised by most rose enthusiasts, however. Don't worry if you make one or two wrong cuts – the roses will probably still bloom prolifically.

1 Moderate pruning is the most appropriate for established hybrid tea roses. Cut back the stems by about half, to an outward-facing bud to keep the centre of the bush open.

2 You can treat floribundas in the same way, but if you prune some shoots severely and others lightly, flowering may be spread over a longer period. Prune the oldest shoots back close to the base, those that grew last year by about a third only.

3 Whichever type of rose you are pruning, cut back any dead or diseased shoots to healthy wood.

START OFF BEGONIA AND GLOXINIA TUBERS

Tuberous-rooted begonias can be grown as pot-plants or in the garden, but wherever they are destined it is well worth starting them into growth now in the greenhouse. This way you will have well-developed plants to put in the garden that will flower much earlier than if the tubers were planted directly into the soil.

Gloxinias, which are suitable only for cultivation in the home or greenhouse, should also be started into growth now.

1 If you are growing your begonias as pot-plants, start them off in small pots to save space in the early stages. Loosely fill the pots with a peat-based or peat-substitute mixture intended for seeds or cuttings.

2 If the tubers have small shoots it will be obvious which is the top, otherwise look for the side with a slight hollow and keep this upwards. Just press the tuber into the compost (soil mix). Keep in a warm, light place, ideally in a greenhouse.

3 If the begonias are intended for outdoors, perhaps in containers or baskets, start them off in trays instead of pots as this will save space.

LEFT: *'Pin-up' is an outstanding single tuberous-rooted begonia that can be raised from seed to flower in its first year or overwintered as a dry tuber.*

4 Gloxinia tubers are started into growth in the same way, but as they will be grown as pot-plants you may prefer to plant them in their final 13–15cm (5–6in) pots. The 'hairy' side (the remains of old roots) is the one to press into the compost.

POT UP AND POT ON CUTTINGS

Pot up cuttings, such as those of pelargoniums and fuchsias, to ensure that their growth rate is not checked. With warmer temperatures they will now be growing vigorously.

1 Pot up the cuttings as soon as they have formed strong root growth. Use an 8–10cm (3–4in) pot and a potting mixture suitable for young plants. Water thoroughly, then keep out of direct sunlight for a couple of days while they recover from the root disturbance.

2 Cuttings that rooted earlier and have already been potted up for a month or more may need moving into larger pots. Check that the roots have filled the potting mixture before you transfer them. If the mixture has lots of white roots, pot on into a larger size.

3 Use a pot a couple of sizes larger, and trickle the same kind of potting mix around the root-ball. Firm well to remove air pockets, and water thoroughly.

ENCOURAGE BUSHY FUCHSIAS

Bush-shaped fuchsias respond well to early 'pruning' and training. You can start as soon as the cuttings have three pairs of leaves.

1 Pinch out the growing tip of your fuchsia cuttings once three pairs of leaves have formed, if you want a bushy shape.

2 New shoots will form after a few weeks, but for really bushy plants pinch out the tips of these sideshoots too. Repeat this process several times throughout spring to encourage well-shaped bushy plants.

SAVING SPACE IN THE GREENHOUSE

Greenhouse space is often a problem at this time of year. If you are growing cuttings for the garden rather than as pot-plants, keep the young plants in small pots rather than potting them on into larger ones. To avoid a check to growth, however, you must feed the young plants regularly to avoid starvation. Move them to a frost-free cold frame as soon as it is warm enough to do so, and allow plenty of space between the plants so that the leaves are not overcrowded.

PRICK OUT SEEDLINGS

Prick out seedlings as soon as they are large enough to handle. If you leave them in their original trays or pots too long, they will quickly become overcrowded and difficult to separate without damage. Some plants are best pricked out into individual pots, but this takes up a lot of space and compost (soil mix) so most bedding plants are pricked out into trays. Instead of pricking out into trays, you can use a modular or cell system, like the one shown here, where each plant has its own pocket of soil, separated from the others. The benefit of this method is that there will be less root disturbance when the plants are eventually put into the garden.

1 Choose a module that suits the size of plant. A small seedling such as ageratum or fibrous-rooted begonia will not need such a large cell as, say, a dahlia. Fill the individual cells loosely with a potting mixture suitable for seedlings.

2 Strike the compost (soil mix) off level with a straight edge, but do not compress it. It will settle lower in the cells once the seedlings have been inserted and watered.

3 Loosen the seedlings in the tray or pot you are pricking out from, and if possible lift them one at a time by their seed leaves. These are the first ones to open, and they are usually smaller and a different shape to the true leaves.

4 Use a tool designed for the purpose, or improvise with something like a pencil or plant label, to make a hole large enough to take the roots with as little bending or disturbance as possible.

5 Gently firm the compost around the roots, being careful not to press too hard. Water thoroughly, then keep the plants out of direct sunlight for a couple of days.

ABOVE: *The white alyssum and bright golden annual rudbeckias are among many colourful annuals to be pricked out now.*

PRICK OUT INTO POTS

Some plants, such as bedding pelargoniums and pot-plants for the greenhouse and home, are best pricked out into individual pots rather than trays or even modules.

1 Fill small pots with potting mixture and firm it lightly, using the base of another pot.

2 Loosen the compost (soil mix) with a dibber or transplanting tool. Hold the seedling by its leaves, not the stem.

3 Make a small hole in the centre of the pot, deep enough to take the roots without damage.

4 While still holding the seedling by a leaf, very gently firm the potting mixture around the roots, using a small dibber or a finger. Don't press too hard as watering will also settle the mixture around the roots.

5 Water carefully so that the potting mixture is settled around the roots without washing the plant out. Keep the seedlings in a warm, humid place out of direct sunlight for a few days.

PRICKING OUT TINY SEEDLINGS

Seedlings are almost always pricked out individually, but there are a few special cases when more than a single seedling is used. Lobelia seedlings are tiny, and individual plants not very substantial, so many gardeners prick out a small group of seedlings together, as shown. Prick out about five or six plants at a time, though the number is not critical. Pricking out tiny seedlings in small groups like this also makes the job much quicker and easier, but it is only recommended for certain plants.

By the time these grow into seedlings large enough to plant out they look like one substantial plant.

6 Writing labels for individual pots is tedious and you probably won't want to do it, yet confusion later is highly probable if you have lots of pots containing different varieties. Group individual varieties into trays, and use just one label.

MID SPRING

FOR MANY GARDENERS, MID SPRING IS the most exciting as well as the busiest time of the year. The garden looks colourful again by this time, seedlings and cuttings are growing fast, and outdoor sowing and planting can begin in earnest. This is often a time to make priorities if it isn't possible to keep up with all those urgent jobs. If you don't know whether something can wait, check in the 'Jobs In Brief' notes for late spring; this may enable you to decide what can be delayed. Plants sown or planted in late spring often catch up with those sown a month earlier if the weather happens to be unseasonably cold during mid spring.

JOBS IN BRIEF

The Flower Garden

❏ Plant and stake herbaceous plants
❏ Dead-head spring-flowering bulbs
❏ Buy seeds and bulbs if you have not already done so
❏ Sow hardy annuals
❏ Feed and mulch beds and borders
❏ Plant out sweet peas raised in pots
❏ Sow sweet peas outdoors
❏ Plant ranunculus tubers
❏ Plant container-grown shrubs
❏ Plant gladioli and summer bulbs
❏ Start mowing the lawn regularly

The Greenhouse and Conservatory

❏ Take softwood cuttings
❏ Pot up pelargonium and fuchsia cuttings rooted earlier
❏ Pot up or pot on into larger pots chrysanthemums rooted earlier
❏ Sow seeds of bedding plants and pot plants
❏ Start begonia and gloxinia tubers into growth
❏ Prick out or pot up seedlings sown earlier
❏ Take dahlia cuttings

TOP LEFT: *Keep softwood cuttings in a warm place.*

TOP RIGHT: *Stake tall herbaceous plants.*

RIGHT: *Rhododendrons are at their best now.*

PLANTS AT THEIR BEST

Amelanchier (shrub/tree)
Bergenia (non-woody evergreen)
Cytisus, various (shrub)
Dicentra (herbaceous)
Doronicum (herbaceous)
Forsythia (shrub)
Helleborus orientalis (herbaceous)
Hyacinthus (bulb)
Magnolia × soulangiana (tree)
Magnolia stellata (shrub)
Mahonia, various (shrub)
Muscari armeniacum (bulb)
Narcissus (bulb)
Primula × polyantha (herbaceous)
Prunus 'Kwanzan' (tree)
Pulsatilla vulgaris (rock plant)
Rhododendron, various (shrub)
Ribes sanguineum (shrub)
Saxifraga, various (rock plant)
Tulipa, various (bulb)

LEFT: *Rhododendrons come in many sizes and colours. Most grow tall, but some are compact enough for a small garden.*

BELOW: *Aubrietas and saxifragas can always be relied upon for a colourful display, set off here by green bergenia and juniper foliage.*

TAKE SOFTWOOD CUTTINGS

Softwood cuttings, which are taken from the new shoots produced this year, root quickly and easily, and you can multiply many of your plants this way. The list below suggests a selection of some of the more popular garden plants you can propagate in this way.

PLANTS TO GROW FROM SOFTWOOD CUTTINGS

The following are just some of the popular plants that can be propagated from softwood cuttings taken now, but there are many more to try. It is always worth experimenting if there is a plant that you want to propagate but are not sure if softwood cuttings are suitable. The chances are that some will root.
Caryopteris
Clematis
Forsythia
Fuchsia
Helichrysum
Kolkwitzia
Lavandula
Pelargonium
Salvia (shrubby types)

1 The exact length of a softwood cutting depends on the plant, and some gardeners prefer variations of the basic technique, but typically the stem is cut off below the third or fourth leaf or pairs of leaves.

2 Trim or pull off the lowest pair of leaves (if the plant has scale-like stipules, such as on a pelargonium, pull off these as well). Trim the base of the stem with a sharp knife, cutting just below a leaf joint.

3 Dip the end of the cutting into a rooting hormone for speedier rooting, although many softwood cuttings root easily without this aid. Most rooting powders contain a fungicide, however, and this also helps to prevent rotting.

4 Make a hole with a dibber or pencil, then insert the cutting and firm the rooting mixture gently around it. Do not force the cutting in as this may damage it. If you have a lot of cuttings, insert several around the edge of each pot – but don't let the leaves touch.

5 Water and place in a propagator. If you do not have a propagator, enclose the cuttings in a plastic bag secured with a twist-tie or elastic band. High humidity is very important for softwood cuttings. Make sure that the leaves are not in contact with the bag.

PLANT A HANGING BASKET

The best hanging baskets are those planted with fairly small plants that are then grown on in a light, frost-free place until it is safe to put them outdoors – perhaps in late spring or early summer. A greenhouse is ideal, but you might also be able to use an enclosed or protected porch. Giving the baskets protection for a few weeks enables the plants to recover from the transplanting before they have to contend with the winds and drier soil and air outdoors.

1 Stand the basket on a large pot or a bucket to keep it stable while planting. Use a wire basket if you want a traditional display with plenty of plants cascading from the sides as well as the top.

2 Water-absorbing crystals can be added to the potting compost (soil mix) to act as a buffer if you are occasionally forgetful about watering your plants. However, they are no substitute for regular, daily watering during dry and hot weather.

3 You can use proprietary liners and make slits for planting, but if making a traditional basket, line it with moss to the level of the first row of plants. Fill the basket with potting compost up to that level, then insert the plants.

4 Add more moss and potting mix and repeat until just below the rim. Use a bold plant for the centre. It may be necessary to remove a little of the potting soil from the root-ball if the plant has been in a large pot.

5 Finally, fill in with plants around the edges. Encourage cascading plants to trail quickly and effectively by planting the root-ball at a slight angle so that the plant tilts slightly towards the edge.

6 Water thoroughly and keep in a warm, sheltered place until the plants are well established. If you do not have hanging facilities in the greenhouse, keep the basket on the support used for planting it up.

PLANT OR SOW SWEET PEAS

Sweet peas sown in the autumn and overwintered in a cold frame, or sown in a greenhouse in mid or late winter, will have made sturdy plants ready to be put out, but it is not too late to sow now – indoors or out – for a late summer display. To spread the period over which you can enjoy sweet peas, it is a good idea to sow at different times.

1 Insert the supports before you plant. For the best blooms, on long, straight stems, the cordon system is best, but it is very labour-intensive. Insert T-shaped posts at each end of the double row. Stretch wires between the cross-pieces and secure 2.1m (7ft) canes to these at 23cm (9in) intervals, sloping them slightly inwards.

2 For general garden display and a mass of flowers, a wigwam of canes is more satisfactory. Incline the canes inwards and tie at the top, or use a proprietary cane holder.

3 Wire or plastic netting fixed to canes to form a circular tower is another efficient way to support tall sweet peas for general garden decoration at the back of a border.

4 Remove a hole, large enough to take the root-ball with minimal disturbance, at the base of each cane, or about 23cm (9in) apart.

5 Sweet pea plants are sometimes sold with a cluster of seedlings in one pot. Always separate these and plant individually. Spread the roots out, cover, then water thoroughly.

6 Support the plants from an early stage. They can be wound in and out of netting, or attached to canes with string or metal split rings.

7 If sowing directly into the soil, sow two or three seeds at each position, and thin to one later if more germinate.

STAKE BORDER PLANTS

Some border plants are prone to wind damage, and sometimes a potentially beautiful plant is flattened or broken by the weather. Early staking means that the plants will usually grow through or over the support, which will then become almost invisible.

1 Proprietary supports like this are very efficient at supporting border plants that are not very tall but have a mass of tallish floppy or fragile flowering stems.

2 Proprietary supports that link together as shown are useful where you have clumps of varying sizes to support. They can be linked together to suit the individual plant.

3 Thin sticks pushed into the ground among and around the plant can be very effective. They may look a little unsightly at first, but once the plant grows you probably won't notice them.

4 Short canes can be used to support plants such as carnations. If you use a stout cane, loop string or twine around it and the plant. Use thinner split canes to keep individual flower stems or groups of stems upright.

ABOVE: *Tall garden canes are an efficient way to support plants with very tall flowering spikes that are vulnerable to wind damage, such as delphiniums. Insert individual canes at an early stage, and tie the spike to it loosely as it grows.*

LATE SPRING

LATE SPRING CAN BE DECEPTIVE. It often seems as though summer has already arrived, yet in cold areas there can be severe late frosts. Take the local climate into account before planting any frost-tender plants outdoors. Even with experience, it can be a gamble as an untypical season might produce surprises.

Judging when frosts are no longer likely is mainly a matter of assessing risk. A good guide is to observe when summer bedding is put out in the local parks. These gardeners will have amassed generations of local knowledge of your area, which is by far the best guide.

JOBS IN BRIEF

The Flower Garden

- ❑ Plant container-grown shrubs
- ❑ Sow hardy annuals
- ❑ Plant herbaceous plants
- ❑ Stake herbaceous plants
- ❑ Plant up a half-basket or wall pot
- ❑ Plant gladioli and summer bulbs
- ❑ Mow the lawn regularly from now on
- ❑ Plant out sweet peas raised in pots
- ❑ Harden off tender bedding plants

The Greenhouse and Conservatory

- ❑ Feed pot-plants and seedlings regularly
- ❑ Pot on young dahlia and chrysanthemum plants if they need it

TOP LEFT: *Place bedding plants in cloches so that they can acclimatize gradually.*

TOP RIGHT: *Place bedding plants in a cold frame a week or two before planting-out time.*

BELOW LEFT: *Plant half-baskets with bold and spectacular plants for an eye-catching display. A half-basket against the wall is ideal if you are trying to introduce colour into a small garden.*

BELOW RIGHT: *Wall pots can be highly decorative in their own right, so it is a good idea to choose more restrained plants for more ornamental ones.*

PLANTS AT THEIR BEST

Aubrieta (rock plant)
Azalea (shrub)
Bergenia (non-woody evergreen)
Calendula, autumn sown (hardy annual)
Cheiranthus (wallflower)
Choisya ternata (shrub)
Clematis montana (shrubby climber)
Crataegus (tree)
Cytisus, various (shrub)
Dicentra (herbaceous)
Fritillaria (bulb)
Genista (shrub)
Laburnum (tree)
Malus (tree)
Paeonia (herbaceous and shrub)
Phlox subulata (rock plant)
Pulsatilla vulgaris (rock plant)
Rhododendron, various (shrub)
Saxifraga, various (rock plant)
Syringa (lilac)
Tulipa, various (bulb)
Wisteria (shrubby climber)

LEFT: *Alliums beneath a laburnum arch.*

BELOW: Fritillaria meleagris.

MAKE UP A HALF-BASKET OR WALL POT

Most people love to have a traditional hanging basket, but they can be disappointing unless cared for lovingly. Even though the basket is planted with an all-round view in mind, the side nearest the wall will perform poorly in comparison with the sunny side unless you turn the basket every

day or two to even up growth. A half-basket or wall pot fixed against the wall can be just as effective, and because it is planted to look good from the front only, it can be just as bold and striking as a conventional basket. Some wall pots are also decorative in their own right.

1 If the half-basket is small, you may prefer to take it down to plant it. However, drill and plug the holes, fix the hooks or screws and try it out on the wall first.

2 Add a drainage layer, such as broken pots or gravel, then partly fill with a potting mixture.

3 If using a wire half-basket, line it with moss and fill with potting mixture to the height of the first layer of plants.

4 Plant the sides, then add more moss and potting soil.

5 Plant the top of the basket with bold and spectacular plants for an eye-catching display.

6 Choose more restrained plants for a very ornamental wall pot that you want to retain as a feature in its own right.

PUTTING OUT WALL BASKETS

Half-baskets and wall pots are difficult to accommodate in the greenhouse or other sheltered and frost-free position, so it is best to wait until frost is very unlikely before planting. If you can give them a week or two in a greenhouse or cold frame, however, the plants will receive less of a check to growth and the display should be more pleasing.

RIGHT: *A genuine old manger has been used for this lavish display. Well-planted large wall pots can be just as striking.*

HARDEN OFF BEDDING PLANTS

Hardening off is a crucial stage for all plants raised indoors or in a greenhouse. If this is done properly the plants will remain sturdy and healthy, but if you move tender plants straight out into hot, dry conditions or cold biting winds outdoors after a cosseted life on the windowsill or greenhouse, losses could be high.

Plants that you buy from shops and garden centres should have been hardened off before you buy them.

1 Place the plants in a cold frame a week or two before planting-out time. Close the top in the evening and on cold days, otherwise ventilate freely. If frost threatens, cover the frame with insulation material or take the plants into a greenhouse or indoors again.

2 If you don't have a cold frame, cloches can be used instead. Ventilate them whenever possible so that the plants become acclimatized while still receiving protection from the worst winds and cold.

3 If you don't have frames or cloches, group the trays or pots together in a sheltered spot outside and cover them with horticultural fleece or a perforated plastic floating cloche. Take them in again if frost is forecast.

SUMMER

Early summer is a time of intense gardening activity. Everything is growing rapidly, in many areas tender plants can be put out, and weeds seem to grow faster than you ever thought possible.
Mid and late summer are times for enjoying the results of your earlier efforts. There are always jobs to be done, of course, but you should also make time to relax.
During a dry summer water shortages can be a problem, but always water thoroughly, as shallow, impatient watering will encourage surface rooting and make the plants even more vulnerable.

OPPOSITE: *Roses are part of the summer scene, but they have even more impact when used with imagination.*

ABOVE: *By using containers, summer colour can be brought to even the most unpromising corner of the garden.*

EARLY SUMMER

EARLY SUMMER IS A TIME WHEN you can relax a little and enjoy seeing the results of all your hard work. But there are still jobs to be done, and pests and diseases are as active as ever. Vigilance and prompt action now will often stop the trouble from spreading out of control.

Although there is always plenty of colour at this time of year, there will be a few weeks when the garden is perhaps not looking at its best. During this period, there is often an interval between the spring-flowering plants dying back and the peak of colour offered by abundant summer bedding.

JOBS IN BRIEF

The Flower Garden

❑ Dead-head border plants regularly
❑ Stake border plants
❑ Finish hardening off and planting out tender bedding plants
❑ Plant up containers and baskets
❑ Plant dahlias
❑ Prune lilac, philadelphus, spiraea and broom
❑ Sow biennials such as wallflowers
❑ Sow hardy annuals
❑ Watch out for signs of mildew and aphids on roses, and spray promptly if they are found
❑ Apply a rose fertilizer once the main flush of flowering is over
❑ Pinch out the growing tip from early-flowering chrysanthemums
❑ Water hanging baskets daily and feed weekly

The Greenhouse and Conservatory

❑ Feed pot-plants regularly
❑ Try biological pest control for greenhouse pests

TOP LEFT: *Use a general-purpose fertilizer to avoid using different foods for different plants.*

TOP RIGHT: *Check pot-plants regularly to make sure they are receiving enough water.*

RIGHT: *Experiment with your container plantings first to help visualize how they will look.*

PLANTS AT THEIR BEST

Alchemilla mollis (herbaceous)
Allium (bulb)
Buddleia globosa (shrub)
Calendula (hardy annual)
Cistus (shrub)
Dianthus (carnations and pinks)
Digitalis (biennial)
Geranium (herbaceous)
Godetia (hardy annual)
Iris germanica hybrids (border irises)
Laburnum (tree)
Lupinus (herbaceous)
Paeonia (herbaceous)
Papaver orientale (herbaceous)
Philadelphus (shrub)
Rosa (most types of rose)
Weigela (shrub)

LEFT: *Early summer is full of promise.*

BELOW: Philadelphus *x* lemoinei.

BOTTOM: Dianthus *'Caesar's Bloody Pink.'*

SUMMER TROUGHS AND WINDOWBOXES

Frost-tender bedding plants can now be planted in all but the coldest areas, but be guided by local conditions. Tubs and troughs packed with summer bedding plants are a sure-fire way to bring pockets of cheerful colour to parts of the garden that would not otherwise be so colourful. Make the most of windowboxes, too, which will brighten the exterior of any home.

1 Windowboxes and troughs can be planted in the same way – but for a windowbox include more trailers than you would for a trough. Always make sure that there are drainage holes, and add a drainage layer such as broken pots or gravel.

2 Half fill the box or trough with a good potting mix – a loam-based one can be used for troughs, but if the windowbox is to be fixed on brackets choose a lightweight mixture based on peat or a peat substitute.

3 Most people prefer a mixed planting, with some trailers and both flowering and foliage plants. Try arranging the plants before actually planting to help visualize how they will look.

SINGLE-SUBJECT PLANTING

Most people plant mixed groups, but sometimes a single-subject planting can look especially striking. Impatiens and begonia are popular plants suitable for this treatment, but be prepared to experiment with others.

Because single-subject plants have an even height, it is important to choose a container that is in proportion to the plants. For example, compact begonias look lost in a deep trough but are in keeping with a shallow windowbox.

4 When the positions look right, insert the plants, firming the compost (soil mix) around each root-ball. Plant more closely than in beds or borders, so avoid using plants that will overpower their neighbours.

5 Water thoroughly after planting, and make sure that the compost never dries out. In warm weather this means watering daily, sometimes more than once.

PLANT UP TUBS AND PATIO POTS

Although all the plants suitable for windowboxes and troughs can be used in tubs and large patio pots, the greater depth of potting soil offers scope for larger and often bolder plants, and the circular shape generally demands an eye-catching plant as a centrepiece. Trailers will enhance a plain container, but if you have a very ornate or decorative pot, it may be best to plant trailers with restraint so that the pot itself remains a feature in its own right.

1 Filled tubs and pots can be very heavy to move, so plant them up where they are to be displayed. Cover the drainage holes with a layer of broken pots, gravel or chipped bark.

2 A loam-based potting mixture is best for most plants, but if the pot is to be used where weight is a consideration, such as on a balcony, use a peat-based mixture.

3 Choose a tall or bold plant for the centre, such as *Cordyline australis* or a fuchsia, or one with large flowers such as the osteospermum which has been used here.

4 Fill in around the base with some bushier but lower-growing plants. Choose bright flowers if the centrepiece is a foliage plant, but place the emphasis on foliage effect if the focal-point is a flowering plant.

5 Cover the surface with a decorative mulch such as chipped bark or cocoa shells if much of the surface is visible (this is worth doing anyway to conserve moisture). Water thoroughly.

ABOVE: *Even a simple poppy can make an impact if the container itself is interesting.*

SOW BIENNIALS AND HARDY PERENNIALS

Biennials such as wallflowers and forget-me-nots are very easy to raise from seed, and because they can be sown outdoors they need very little attention. Border perennials such as lupins and aquilegias are also easily raised from seed sown now, and some of them may even flower next summer. Others may take another year or so to establish before flowering.

1 Prepare the ground thoroughly, and eliminate as many weeds as possible. Competition from weeds is often the greatest enemy the seedlings face. Break the soil down into a fine, crumbly structure once it has been cleared of weeds.

2 Take out drills with the corner of a hoe or rake to the recommended depth (this varies with the seed, so check the packet). The drills can be quite close together, because the seedlings will be transplanted as soon as they are large enough.

3 Run water into the drill before sowing if the soil is very dry. Space the seeds thinly, and as evenly as you can. This makes thinning and later transplanting much easier.

4 Cover the seeds by shuffling the soil back with your feet or carefully ease the soil back with the back of a rake. Remember to add a label.

5 Thin the seedlings as soon as they are large enough to handle easily so that they do not become overcrowded.

ABOVE: *Wallflowers are one of the most popular biennials, and really easy to grow from seeds sown now.*

PRUNE SHRUBS

Many shrubs thrive without routine annual pruning, but some that flower in spring or early summer benefit from pruning soon after they have finished flowering. These include *Cytisus* (brooms), *Syringas* (lilacs), philadelphus, and spring-flowering spiraeas.

RENOVATING AN OLD LILAC

1 Philadelphus (illustrated) and spring-flowering spiraeas such as *Spiraea × arguta* and *S. thunbergii* become too dense and overcrowded if they are not pruned. Annual pruning keeps them compact and flowering well, and the best time to do this is immediately after flowering.

2 Reduce the shoots by one-third, cutting out the oldest ones. Cut back the old stems to where a new shoot is growing lower down, or to just above the ground if the shoot is very old and the bush very congested.

Very old *Syringa vulgaris* varieties often become tall and leggy, with the flowers very high up. You may be able to rejuvenate a neglected plant by sawing it down to a height of 30–90cm (12in–3ft). This sounds drastic, and it will not flower for a year or two, but it should shoot from the old wood and produce an attractive compact plant again.

3 Brooms and genistas tend to become woody at the base with age, with the flowers too high up the plants to look attractive. Prune them as soon as the flowers die and the seed pods are beginning to form.

4 Cut back each shoot to about half way along the new green growth. Do not count dark, old wood, and do not cut back into this as new shoots will be reluctant to grow. You will not be able to make an old neglected plant bush from the base – start regular pruning from an early stage.

5 Lilacs benefit from careful deadheading. As soon as the flowering is over, cut the dead blooms back to the first pair of leaves below the flower head (no further, otherwise you might remove buds from which new flowering shoots will be produced).

FEEDING AND WATERING IN THE GREENHOUSE

Watering is a year-round chore in the greenhouse, but the summer months are even more demanding. Consider an automatic or semi-automatic watering system to make lighter work of the job. Most pot-plants respond readily to regular feeding during the growing season, but underfeeding is not easy to detect until the plants have been starved for some time.

1 Plants should be watered before they show obvious signs of distress such as wilting. With bushy plants it is not possible to judge by the visual appearance of the potting mixture either, and touch is often the only practical guide. However, this is both time-consuming and only reasonably accurate.

2 Moisture indicators for individual pots can be helpful for a beginner, or if there are just a few plants, but they are not a practical solution if you have a whole greenhouse or conservatory full of plants.

3 Capillary matting is an ideal way to water most pot-plants in summer. You can use a proprietary system fed by mains (faucet) water, or improvize with a system like the one illustrated. This uses a length of gutter for the water supply. Keep it topped up by hand, with special water bags or from a cistern.

4 If watering by hand, use the can without a rose unless you are watering seedlings. This will enable you to direct water more easily to the roots rather than sprinkling the leaves. Use a finger over the end of the spout to control the flow, or stick a rag in the end to break the force.

5 An overhead spray system operated automatically or when you turn on the tap is useful for a large greenhouse, either for plants on benches or those planted in the border. Water is not so carefully directed to where it is needed, so it is not ideal for pot-plants, but the spray helps to create a humid atmosphere.

6 Use a liquid fertilizer applied with the water if you can remember to do it regularly. There are both soluble powders and liquids that can be diluted to the appropriate strength.

7 Fertilizer sticks and tablets that you push into the potting soil are a convenient way to administer fertilizer if you don't want to apply liquid feeds regularly. Most of these release their nutrients over a period of several months.

Use a general-purpose fertilizer if you want to avoid using different foods for different plants: this is better than not feeding at all.

Some fertilizers are described as being specially formulated for either foliage plants or flowering plants, however, and these will suit the majority of plants within each category. But if you have to feed both flowering and foliage plants with the one fertilizer, these are unlikely to do any harm.

Some enthusiasts prefer to use special feeds for certain types of plant, such as saintpaulias and cacti, but these will also respond to fertilizers used for other pot-plants.

Fertilizers formulated for strong feeders such as tomatoes and chrysanthemums should only be used on other plants with care – they may be too strong.

BIOLOGICAL CONTROLS

The greenhouse or conservatory is an ideal place to practise biological control methods – the predators will thrive in the protected environment, and should multiply rapidly until control is achieved.

1 Various forms of biological controls are available for a number of greenhouse pests. *Encarsia formosa* is a tiny wasp that parasitizes whitefly larvae and eventually kills them. There are other predatory wasps and mites that will attack red spider, soft scale insects and thrips.

2 If weevil grubs destroy your plants by eating the roots, try controlling them in future with a parasitic eelworm. A suspension of the eelworms is simply watered over the potting soil in each pot.

WORKING WITH BIOLOGICAL CONTROLS

Biological controls usually work best when the weather is warm, and some are unsuitable for use outdoors. Use pesticides with care, as they can wipe out your predators as well as the harmful insects and you will destroy the balance between the two.

With biological controls you will always have some pests – they are essential for the predator to be able to continue to breed – but only at a low population level.

MID SUMMER

MID SUMMER IS MAINLY A TIME to enjoy your garden, rather than do a lot of physical work in it. Most things are already sown or planted, and the emphasis is on weeding and watering. Regular dead-heading will keep the garden looking tidy and the plants will benefit too.

JOBS IN BRIEF

The Flower Garden

- ❑ Dead-head border plants regularly
- ❑ Hoe beds and borders regularly to keep down weeds
- ❑ Take semi-ripe cuttings
- ❑ Layer shrubs and carnations
- ❑ Divide and replant border irises
- ❑ Order bulb catalogues and bulbs for autumn delivery
- ❑ Disbud early-flowering chrysanthemums
- ❑ Transplant biennials and perennial seedlings to a nursery bed
- ❑ Mow lawns except in dry weather
- ❑ Watch out for signs of mildew and aphids on roses and spray promptly if found

The Greenhouse and Conservatory

- ❑ Water plants daily
- ❑ Feed pot-plants regularly
- ❑ Look out for pests and diseases Spray promptly or try a biological control for greenhouse pests
- ❑ Feed chrysanthemums regularly

TOP LEFT: *Layering shrubs usually produces fewer but bigger plants.*

TOP RIGHT: *Disbud chrysanthemums during mid summer if you want larger flowers later.*

BELOW LEFT: *Do not forget to feed. Slow-release sticks like the one shown here make it a less frequent chore.*

BELOW RIGHT: *Divide flag irises after flowering and if the rhizomes have become very congested.*

PLANTS AT THEIR BEST

Alchemilla mollis (herbaceous)
Althaea (herbaceous)
Astilbe (herbaceous)
Cistus (shrub)
Clematis (shrubby climber)
Dianthus (carnations and pinks)
Digitalis (biennial)
Geranium (herbaceous)
Hardy annuals (many)
Helianthemum (shrub)
Hydrangea (shrub)
Hypericum (shrub)
Kniphofia (herbaceous)
Lavandula (shrub)
Lilium (bulb)
Potentilla (shrub)
Rosa (most types of rose)
Summer bedding
Verbascum (herbaceous)

ABOVE: *Lilies like this 'Connecticut King' make stunning border plants.*

BELOW: *Mid summer sees the garden at its most beautiful.*

TAKE SEMI-RIPE CUTTINGS

Semi-ripe cuttings – also known as semi-mature cuttings – can be used to propagate a wide range of shrubs, both hardy and tender. If you take them in mid or late summer most will root quickly, and in the case of hardy plants you don't even need a propagator.

1 Choose shoots that are almost fully grown except for the soft tip. The base of the cutting should be hardening, even though the tip may still be soft. Most cuttings are best made 5–10cm (2–4in) long.

2 Strip the lower leaves from each plant to leave a short length of clear stem to insert into the soil.

3 It is well worth using a rooting hormone. Dip the cut end into the powder, liquid or gel, but if using a powder dip the ends into water first so that the powder adheres.

4 Cuttings taken from hardy plants will root outside at this time of year, though they will perform better in a cold frame or propagator.

5 Firm the cuttings to ensure there are no large pockets of air, which might cause the new roots to dry out.

6 Remember to insert a label. This is especially important if you are rooting a number of different kinds of shrubs.

SOME SHRUBS TO PROPAGATE FROM SEMI-RIPE CUTTINGS

Buddleia	Fuchsia
Camellia	Griselinia
Ceanothus	Hebe
Choisya	Hydrangea
Cistus	Philadelphus
Cotoneaster	Potentilla
(illustrated)	Pyracantha
Escallonia	Rosemary
Forsythia	Weigela

7 Water thoroughly. It is worth adding a fungicide to the water initially, to reduce the chance of the cuttings rotting. Make sure that the soil does not dry out at any time.

LAYER SHRUBS

Layering is usually used for shrubby plants that have low branches easily pegged to the ground, but a few border plants can also be layered – carnations and pinks are often raised this way. In comparison with cuttings, layers usually produce fewer but bigger plants.

1 Find a low-growing shoot that can easily be pegged down to the ground. Trim off the leaves just from the area that will be in contact with the soil.

2 Bend the stem down until it touches the ground. Make a hole 10cm (4in) deep, sloping toward the parent plant but with the other side vertical.

3 Twist or slit the stem slightly to injure it. Peg it into the hole with a piece of bent wire or a peg, using the vertical back of the excavation to force the shoot upright.

4 Return the soil and firm it well. If you keep the ground moist, roots should form and within 12–18 months you may be able to sever the new plant from its parent.

DIVIDE FLAG IRISES

Divide flag irises – hybrids derived from *Iris germanica* – after flowering and if the rhizomes have become very congested.

1 Lift the clump with a fork, and cut away and discard the oldest parts. Use only the current season's growth for replanting.

2 Trim the leaves to stumps about 5–8cm (2–3in) long. Replant the pieces of rhizome on a slight ridge of soil, covering the roots but leaving the tops exposed.

LAYERING CARNATIONS

Border carnations and pinks are layered in a similar way to shrubs, but root much more quickly. Select a few well-spaced, non-flowering shoots and remove all but the top four or five leaves on them. Make a small slit in each one with a sharp knife below the lowest pair of leaves, and peg the shoot – slit down – into good soil. Keep moist.

LATE SUMMER

LATE SUMMER IS USUALLY A TIME of hot, dry weather, when there is a natural lull in the garden, and the efforts of spring and early summer sowing and planting will have paid their dividends. The chores that need to be carried out in early autumn can wait until the holidays are over and cooler weather begins to return. Most of this month's work in the garden involves watering and other routine tasks such as mowing the lawn, hoeing beds and borders, and clipping hedges.

JOBS IN BRIEF

The Flower Garden

- ❑ Dead-head plants regularly
- ❑ Feed plants in containers to keep the blooms coming
- ❑ Hoe beds and borders regularly
- ❑ Order bulb catalogues and bulbs
- ❑ Take fuchsia and pelargonium cuttings
- ❑ Prune rambler roses
- ❑ Take semi-ripe cuttings
- ❑ Water the lawn in dry spells, but a few good soaks will be better than many sprinklings
- ❑ Watch out for pests and diseases on roses and other vulnerable plants
- ❑ Feed and disbud dahlias and chrysanthemums as necessary
- ❑ Keep paths and drives weed-free

The Greenhouse and Conservatory

- ❑ Feed pot-plants regularly
- ❑ Watch out for pests and diseases
- ❑ Take semi-ripe cuttings

TOP LEFT: *Fork over the ground before planting.*

TOP RIGHT: *Rosemary provides a delightful display of flowers as well as a fresh supply of culinary seasonings.*

BELOW LEFT: *In the greenhouse, plant prepared hyacinths for early flowering.*

BELOW RIGHT: *If in doubt about how to plant a specific bulb, just plant it on its side.*

PLANTS AT THEIR BEST

Dahlia (bulb)
Erigeron (herbaceous)
Fuchsia (shrub)
Helenium (herbaceous)
Hibiscus syriacus (shrub)
Hydrangea (shrub)
Hypericum (shrub)
Lavatera (shrub)
Lilium (bulb)
Perovskia atriplicifolia (shrub)
Romneya (shrub)
Solidago (herbaceous)
Summer bedding
Verbascum (herbaceous)

RIGHT: *Fuchsias flower throughout the summer and will continue into autumn.*

BELOW: Perovskia atriplicifolia *'Blue Spire' is one of the best blue flowers for late summer, and is undemanding to grow.*

TAKE FUCHSIA CUTTINGS

Fuchsias are really easy to root, and by taking cuttings now you will have young plants that can be overwintered in a light position in a cool but frost-free room or in a greenhouse. These will make good plants for next summer, or you can use them to provide more cuttings next spring.

1 Softwood cuttings can be taken for as long as new growth is being produced, but at this time of year semi-ripe (semi-mature) cuttings root easily and are simple to take. Pull off sideshoots about 10cm (4in) long, with a 'heel' of old main stem attached.

2 Trim off the lowest leaves and trim the end of the heel to make a clean cut. If you have taken cuttings without a heel, trim the stem straight across beneath a leaf-joint.

3 Although cuttings will usually root without aid, a hormone rooting powder should speed the process. Insert several cuttings around the edge of an 8–10cm (3–4in) pot filled with a rooting mixture.

4 Label the cuttings, water and place in a cold frame or greenhouse, or on a window-sill. Keep the compost (soil mix) damp, and pot up individually when well rooted. Protect from frost.

TAKE PELARGONIUM CUTTINGS

Pelargoniums (popularly known as bedding geraniums) can be overwintered in a frost-free place to provide cuttings next spring. Many experts prefer to take cuttings now, however, and to overwinter the young plants in a light, frost-free place.

RIGHT: *Pelargoniums, or bedding geraniums, are one of the most popular of summer plants.*

1 Take cuttings from non-flowering shoots (if you have to use flowering shoots, cut off the blooms). A good guide to length is to cut the shoot off just above the third joint below the growing tip.

2 Remove the lowest pair of leaves with a sharp knife, and remove any flowers or buds. Trim straight across the base of each cutting, just below the lowest leaf joint. You can dip the ends in a rooting hormone, but they usually root readily without.

3 Insert about five cuttings around the edge of a 13cm (5in) pot containing a cuttings mixture and firm gently. Keep in a light, warm position but out of direct sun. Be careful not to overwater, otherwise the cuttings will rot. Pot up individually when rooted.

DAHLIA AND CHRYSANTHEMUM CARE

Dahlias and chrysanthemums come into their true glory at the end of summer and into autumn, just as most flowers have passed their best. Some types are simply left to produce masses of blooms with no intervention, but those grown for large flowers are usually selectively disbudded. This produces fewer but larger blooms. Both types of plant need plenty of feeding and a careful watch has to be kept to prevent pests and diseases marring these plants.

1 To produce larger flowers, pinch out the side buds behind the crown (central) flower bud of dahlias, while they are still small. Many chrysanthemums are also disbudded, but how and when you do it depends on the variety, so be guided by a specialist catalogue or publication.

2 The best way to control pests and diseases is to spray at the first signs. Often it may be possible to prevent spread simply by pinching off and destroying the first few affected leaves. This chrysanthemum shows evidence of leaf miner damage.

3 Chrysanthemums and dahlias benefit from regular feeding. Even if you used a slow-release fertilizer to see them through most of the summer, they will probably respond to a boost now. Use a quick-acting general fertilizer or a high-potash feed, but don't boost with too much nitrogen.

PLANT BULBS FOR SPRING

Spring-flowering bulbs are now widely available, but exactly when you plant them will depend largely on whether the ground has been cleared of summer plants. If planting in beds, it is best to let summer bedding flower for as long as possible, and you may prefer not to disturb the last of the summer colour in herbaceous borders just yet, but in vacant ground it is best to plant as soon as possible. Bulbs are always better in the ground rather than in bags and boxes that are probably stored in less than ideal conditions. Bulbs look good in front of shrubs, and you should be able to plant these as soon as they are obtainable. Indoor bulbs that are specially prepared for early flowering should also be planted as soon as they become available.

1 Fork over the ground before planting, and if the plants are to be left undisturbed for some years, try to incorporate plenty of organic material such as rotted garden compost or manure. Many bulbs like well-drained soil but still benefit from plenty of organic material that will hold moisture and nutrients.

2 Avoid adding quick-acting fertilizers in the autumn. Controlled-release fertilizers that provide nutrients according to the soil temperature can be used, but they are best employed in spring. Instead rake a very slow-acting fertilizer such as bonemeal, which contains mainly phosphate, into the surface, or apply it to the planting holes.

3 Where there is space and the plants will benefit from planting in an informal group or cluster, dig out a hole about three times the depth of the bulbs and wide enough to take the clumps.

4 Space the bulbs so that they look like a natural clump. Use the spacing recommended on the packet as a guide. Wide spacing will allow for future growth and multiplication, but if you intend to lift the bulbs after flowering much closer spacing will create a bolder display.

5 Draw the soil back over the bulbs, being careful not to dislodge them in the process.

6 Firm the soil with the back of the rake rather than treading it, which may damage the bulbs.

7 If you are likely to cultivate the area before the shoots come through, mark out where bulbs have been planted with a few small canes. Always insert a label, as it will be months before the bulbs appear and flower, by which time it is often difficult to remember the variety planted.

RECOGNIZING WHICH WAY UP TO PLANT BULBS

Most bulbs have a very obvious top and bottom and present no problem. Others, especially tubers, can cause confusion because they lack an obvious growing point. If in doubt, just plant them on their side – the shoot will grow upwards and the roots down.

A few bulbs that do have an obvious top are planted on their side because the base tends to rot in wet soil, though these are rare exceptions. *Fritillaria imperialis* is sometimes planted this way, and it is always worth planting vulnerable bulbs on a bed of grit or coarse sand to encourage good drainage around the base, as shown.

PLANTING IN INDIVIDUAL HOLES

If you have a lot of bulbs to plant over a wide area, individual planting holes may be more appropriate than creating larger excavations to take a group of bulbs.

There are special long-handled planting tools, but an ordinary long-handled trowel is just as good. You can use a normal trowel with a handle of conventional length, but it makes planting more tedious if the area is large.

Check periodically to make sure that the holes are being made to the correct depth. After checking a few it will be easy to judge by eye.

Make a hole large enough to take the bulb easily (it must not become wedged in the hole, as the roots will then be exposed to dry air).

Return the excavated soil. If planting a large area, you can shuffle it back in with your feet, then rake the surface level.

ABOVE: *Tulips, wallflowers and forget-me-nots, all ideal for spring bedding.*

Autumn

Be watchful and vigilant as the nights become colder. In some areas quite severe frosts are common in early autumn, and in others light frosts may not occur until mid or late autumn, if at all. Listen to the weather forecasts and take in or protect vulnerable plants if frost is expected. Think seriously about winter protection for plants on the borderline of hardiness, and be prepared to give early winter shelter, perhaps in the form of a windbreak, for newly planted evergreens. A little protection can ensure that many plants survive instead of succumbing to winter winds and cold.

OPPOSITE: *The colourful leaves of* Rhus typhina *'Laciniata', with the white plumes of a cortaderia in the background.*

ABOVE: Liriope muscari, *one of the delights of autumn, is fortunately tough and very easy to grow.*

EARLY AUTUMN

THE WEATHER IN EARLY AUTUMN IS still warm enough to make outdoor gardening a comfortable experience, and although the vibrant flowers of summer may be gone, there are plenty of delights still to be enjoyed in the form of bright berries and flaming foliage, not to mention late-flowering gems such as chrysanthemums and nerines. Apart from bulb planting for next spring, and protecting frost-tender plants, there are few really pressing jobs at this time of year.

JOBS IN BRIEF

The Flower Garden

- ❑ Plant spring-flowering bulbs
- ❑ Take fuchsia and pelargonium cuttings
- ❑ Plant lilies
- ❑ Clear summer bedding and prepare for spring bedding plants
- ❑ Continue to watch for pests and diseases on roses and other vulnerable plants
- ❑ Disbud dahlias and chrysanthemums as necessary
- ❑ Lift and store dahlias after the first frost
- ❑ Lift and store gladioli and other tender bulbs, corms and tubers

The Greenhouse and Conservatory

- ❑ Bring in house and greenhouse plants that have been standing outdoors for the summer
- ❑ Clean off any summer shading washes that you applied
- ❑ Check that greenhouse heaters are in good working order. Arrange to have them serviced, if necessary

TOP LEFT: *Fork over the ground after clearing it of summer bedding plants.*

TOP RIGHT: *Feeding lilies planted in early autumn is crucial.*

RIGHT: *When lifting plants from a nursery bed take as much soil around the roots as possible.*

PLANTS AT THEIR BEST

Anemone japonica (herbaceous)
Aster novae-angliae (herbaceous)
Aster novi-belgii (herbaceous)
Chrysanthemum, early-flowering garden type (herbaceous)
Dahlia (bulb)
Hibiscus syriacus (shrub)
Hydrangea (shrub)
Lavatera (shrub)
Nerine bowdenii (bulb)
Pyracantha, berries (shrub)
Rudbeckia (herbaceous)
Sedum spectabile (herbaceous)
Solidago (herbaceous)
Sorbus, berries (tree)
Sternbergia lutea (bulb)

RIGHT: *The autumn-flowering* Sedum spectabile *is a highlight of autumn.*

BELOW: *Rudbeckia fulgida 'Goldsturm' is one of the stars of the autumn border.*

PLANT UP A SPRING WINDOWBOX WITH BULBS

Spring bulb displays are less predictable than summer flowers, and it can be especially disappointing when different bulbs planted in the same windowbox flower at different times. The consolation is that this does at least extend the interest. A good alternative is to plant single-subject displays which, although often brief, are frequently bolder.

1 Make sure that there are drainage holes, and add a layer of material to aid quick drainage, such as broken pots or pieces of chipped bark (sold for mulching).

2 Add enough potting soil to cover the bottom couple of centimetres (about an inch). As the bulbs do not need a lot of nutrients during the winter, you can often use some of the potting mixture previously used for summer bedding.

3 You can pack in more bulbs by planting in layers. Place large bulbs such as daffodils or tulips at the lower level.

4 Add more potting soil, then position the smaller bulbs, such as crocuses and scillas. Try to position them so that they lie between the larger bulbs. Be careful about the bulbs that you mix – small crocuses will be swamped by tall daffodils, so choose miniature or dwarf daffodils, to keep a suitable balance.

5 Top up with more potting soil, but leave 2–3cm (¾–1in) of space at the top for watering and perhaps a decorative mulch. As the windowbox will look bare for some months, a few winter pansies will add a touch of interest. Don't worry about the bulbs beneath – they will find their way through the pansies.

BULBS AND SPRING BEDDING

Some of the best container displays for spring combine bulbs with spring-flowering bedding plants such as forget-me-nots (*Myosotis*), double daisies (*Bellis*) and cultivated primroses. This is often more effective than filling the container with bulbs alone. It means that the container looks less bleak after planting, and the period of flowering is greatly extended.

Put the plants in first, then the bulbs between them. If you plant the bulbs first, it will be difficult to remember the positioning and they are likely to be disturbed when you insert the plants.

LEFT: *Even common plants like tulips and pansies can look stunning in the right combination and setting.*

PLANT UP A TUB OR PATIO POT WITH BULBS

Tubs, large pots, and urns can be planted in the same way as windowboxes – with bulbs in multiple layers or combined with spring-flowering plants – but bulbs also make good companions for shrubs and small trees in tubs.

They make the most of space around the edge of the container that is usually wasted, and if the shrubby plant sheds its leaves in winter, the bulbs will complete the important parts of their annual cycle before there is competition for light.

1 If planting an empty container, try placing a small conifer in the centre to provide winter interest. A few ivies positioned so that they trail over the edge will usually improve the appearance in winter.

2 Position the bulbs on the surface first so that they are evenly spaced around the edge. Small plants that multiply freely, such as *Muscari armeniacum*, scillas, chionodoxas, and *Anemone blanda*, are among the plants that can usually be depended upon to improve year by year.

3 Plant with a trowel, being careful to disturb the roots of an established plant as little as possible.

PLANT BEDS AND BORDERS FOR A SPRING DISPLAY

Beds normally used for summer bedding can be replanted with spring bedding – a combination of plants and bulbs will create a better display than bulbs alone. Plants like forget-me-nots and double daisies help to clothe the ground between the bulbs during the winter, and in spring fill in around the base of tall bulbs such as tulips that can otherwise look rather stalky.

It is a good idea to see what your local parks department does for plant combinations. It is better to modify an existing combination that you like, even if you don't want to copy it exactly, rather than experiment if you don't know much about the plants. A failure will mean that you will have to wait another year for the next attempt.

1 Fork over the ground after clearing it of summer bedding plants. Fertilizer is not normally needed, but bonemeal, which is very slow-acting, is worth adding if the soil is impoverished. Apply bonemeal after forking over and rake it in.

2 If you have raised the plants yourself, and have them growing in a nursery bed, water well about an hour before lifting them. Lift with as much soil round the roots as possible.

3 Spring bedding plants bought from garden centres are usually sold in trays or strips. These are usually disposable, so don't be afraid to break them if this allows you to release the root-ball with as little damage as possible.

ABOVE: *Tulips usually look better if underplanted with wallflowers or forget-me-nots.*

4 Space the plants out on the surface, allowing for the bulbs, before planting. Space the bulbs out, then begin planting from the back or one end.

PLANT LILIES FOR SUMMER

Lilies are often planted in spring, but you can also plant them now except in very cold areas. The bulbs are less likely to dry out, which can result in failures. Most lilies prefer a slightly acid soil (pH6–6.5), but some – including *Lilium candidum* – will do well in alkaline soils.

1 Lilies demand a well-prepared site, so dig the soil deeply and work in as much well-rotted manure or garden compost as you can spare. Add plenty of grit to improve drainage if the soil tends to be wet.

2 Lilies look best in groups rather than as isolated specimens, so excavate an area of soil to a depth of about 20cm (8in), large enough to take at least four or five bulbs. Add coarse grit or sand unless the soil is very well drained.

3 Add a sprinkling of bonemeal or a controlled-release fertilizer, as lilies are usually left undisturbed until overcrowded and therefore feeding is more important than with bedding bulbs used for a single season.

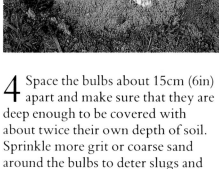

4 Space the bulbs about 15cm (6in) apart and make sure that they are deep enough to be covered with about twice their own depth of soil. Sprinkle more grit or coarse sand around the bulbs to deter slugs and reduce the risk of waterlogging.

5 Place small canes or sticks around the planting area before you return the soil. These remind you to avoid damaging the emerging shoots when you hoe. Remember to label.

ABOVE: *Lilies are real eye-catchers, as this drift of the compact 'Little Girl' proves.*

CLEAR SUMMER BEDDING

If frosts have not put an abrupt end to your summer bedding display, the plants will undoubtedly be looking sad and dejected by now.

Even if you do not plan to replant with spring bedding, the garden will look tidier if the old plants are cleared away and the ground dug over.

1 Plants like this will do more good on the compost heap than left on show. Bare soil can look neat and tidy provided you eliminate weeds.

2 Bedding plants generally have shallow roots and are easy to pull up by hand. If some are deep-rooted, just loosen the roots with a fork.

3 Old bedding plants are ideal for the compost heap. Being non-woody they rot down easily.

4 Dig over the ground, and remove any large weeds. Use a spade if the ground is very weedy so that most of them can be buried as the soil is turned, otherwise use a fork.

5 Whether or not you are replanting with spring bedding, rake the ground level so that it looks neat and tidy.

PRESERVE AND STORE GARDEN CANES

Bamboo canes deteriorate after a season or two in use, especially where they have been in the ground. Extend their life by cleaning and preserving them. Store in a dry place, rather than leaving them exposed in the garden.

1 Knock most of the soil off, then scrub the canes with a stiff brush and garden or household disinfectant. Pay special attention to the ends, and make sure any soil is removed.

2 Wipe the scrubbed canes with a cloth to dry them, then stand the ends that have been in the soil in a bucket or container partly filled with a wood preservative. Leave overnight to allow the preservative to penetrate.

3 Bundle the canes to keep them tidy, and store in a dry place until needed next year.

LIFT AND STORE GLADIOLI

Gladioli can only be left in the ground in mild areas where frosts are always light and do not penetrate far into the soil. In cold areas gladioli will be killed if they remain in the soil, so lift them before there are penetrating frosts.

Gladioli flower reliably from year to year, so they are almost always worth saving. The cormels (small corms) that form around the base will reach flowering size within a couple of years if looked after.

1 Loosen the soil with a garden fork before attempting to lift the plants.

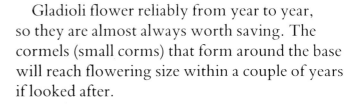

2 Trim off most of the foliage, leaving just a stub to dry off. Shake off most of the soil.

3 Leave the lifted plants in a dry place for a few days to dry off. When the remains of the old stems have shrivelled, trim them off, and remove the cormels that have grown around the base. Store these if you want to save them, otherwise discard. Pull off the remains of the old corm to leave just the healthy new corm. Lay the corms in trays and keep in a frost-proof place for a day or two for further drying.

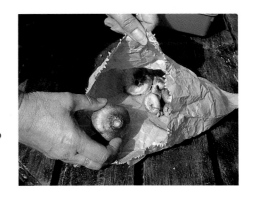

4 Dust with fungicide and store in paper bags away from frost.

MID AUTUMN

THIS IS AN UNPREDICTABLE TIME of the year. In cold regions quite severe frosts are not uncommon, while in mild climates some plants are still growing and tender plants may not be brought to an abrupt end for another month or more.

This is a time to listen to the weather forecast and to be on the alert, in particular, for frost warnings if you haven't yet had the first frost of the season. Be flexible and garden with an eye to the weather as well as the calendar.

JOBS IN BRIEF

The Flower Garden

- ❑ Plant roses
- ❑ Plant spring bulbs
- ❑ Plant bare-root and balled trees and shrubs
- ❑ Plant herbaceous plants
- ❑ Divide overlarge herbaceous plants
- ❑ Clear summer bedding
- ❑ Take in tender fuchsias and pelargoniums
- ❑ Protect vulnerable plants
- ❑ Cut down and lift dahlias blackened by frost
- ❑ Lift and take in chrysanthemums not hardy enough to overwinter
- ❑ Lift gladioli corms
- ❑ Plant lilies
- ❑ Sow sweet peas in pots
- ❑ Collect and compost fallen leaves

The Greenhouse and Conservatory

- ❑ Clean and disinfect for winter
- ❑ Insulate
- ❑ Remove yellowing and dead leaves from plants
- ❑ Check minimum temperatures are achieved and that heaters work
- ❑ Ventilate whenever mild enough

TOP LEFT: *Use large pots to overwinter pelargoniums.*

TOP RIGHT: *Cover outdoor fuchsias with straw.*

RIGHT: *Store dahlia tubers in a well-insulated box in a frost-free location.*

PLANTS AT THEIR BEST

Acer, colourful foliage (tree/shrub)
Anemone japonica (herbaceous)
Aster novi-belgii (herbaceous)
Berberis, colourful foliage and berries
(shrub)
Fothergilla, colourful foliage (shrub)
Liriope muscari (herbaceous)
Parthenocissus, colourful foliage
(climber)
Pernettya, berries (shrub)
Pyracantha, berries (shrub)
Schizostylis coccinea (herbaceous)

LEFT: *Apples are very decorative fruits, and some will be ready to harvest.*

BELOW LEFT: Parthenocissus tricuspidatus *ends its season with brilliant autumn colour.*

BELOW: *'Audrey' is one of many varieties of* Aster novi-belgii, *ideal for autumn colour.*

NATURALIZE BULBS IN GRASS

Naturalizing bulbs is a good way to enjoy a trouble-free display each spring, and one that should improve each year. You will need an area of grass that you don't mind leaving unmown until early summer, to allow bulb foliage to die back naturally.

1 If you have a lot of small bulbs, such as crocuses and eranthis, to plant in a limited area, try lifting an area of turf. Use a spade or half-moon edger to make an H-shaped cut.

2 Slice beneath the grass with a spade until you can fold the turf back for planting.

3 Loosen the ground first, as it will be very compacted. If you want to apply a slow-acting fertilizer such as bonemeal, work it into the soil at the same time.

4 Avoid planting in rows or regimented patterns. You want them to look natural and informal, so scatter them and plant where they fall.

5 If you plant large bulbs this way, you will have to make deeper holes with a trowel. Plant them so that they are covered with about twice their own depth of soil.

6 Firm the soil then return the grass. Firm again if necessary to make sure it is flat, and water if the weather is dry to ensure that the grass grows again quickly.

7 Large bulbs such as daffodils are easier to plant using a bulb planter that takes out a core of soil. Scatter the bulbs randomly so that the display will look natural.

8 Push the bulb planter into the soil, twisting it a little if the ground is hard, then pull it out with the core of soil. Release the core of soil and place the bulb at the bottom of the hole.

9 First pull off a little soil from the base of the core (to allow for the depth of the bulb), then replace the core in the hole. Firm gently.

RIGHT: Try naturalizing bulbs, like these anemones, at the edge of the lawn, where you can leave the grass long until the plants die down.

LIFT AND STORE DAHLIAS

Do not discard your dahlias – lift the tubers before frosts penetrate the ground, and store them for next year. Even seed-raised plants will have formed tubers that you can store.

1 Lift the dahlia tubers once the first frosts have blackened the foliage. Use a fork to lift the tubers, to minimize the risk of damaging them. Cut off the old stem to leave a stump about 5cm (2in) long.

2 Stand the tubers upside down so that moisture drains easily from the hollow stems. Using a mesh support is a convenient way to allow them to dry off. Keep in a dry, frost-free place.

3 After a few days the tubers should be dry enough to store. Remove surplus soil, trim off loose bits of old roots and shorten the stem to leave a short stump. Label each plant.

4 Pack the tubers in a well-insulated box with peat, vermiculite, wood shavings, or crumpled newspaper placed between them. Keep in a frost-free location.

WINTER QUARTERS

A spare bedroom or cool but frost-free garage are sensible places to store overwintering bulbs, corms and tubers such as dahlias. Avoid a very warm place, as roots will spread more rapidly if they become established, and the bulbs or tubers are more likely to dry out. Keep bulbs, corms and tubers where you can easily check them about once a month, to ensure they are all still sound. Any that start to rot must be removed immediately.

PROTECT VULNERABLE SHRUBS

Many shrubs on the borderline of hardiness can be coaxed through the winter with a little protection. There are several methods you can use to provide shelter.

1 A little protection from cold winds and snow is all that many cold-sensitive shrubs require in areas where they are of borderline hardiness. Push cut branches of evergreens, such as conifers, into the soil around the plant.

2 If the shrub is tall, you may also need to tie cut branches of evergreens, or bracken, so that they remain in position.

3 If you don't have a supply of evergreen shoots or bracken, use horticultural fleece or a woven mesh for protection. For extra protection, fold these over to give more than one thickness before tying into position.

4 Some shrubs are damaged by cold winds as much as low temperatures, and for these a windbreak will prevent wind scorch. Insert canes or stakes around the plant, then fix several layers of wind-break netting or plastic sheeting to these.

RIGHT: *Always knock heavy falls of snow off your conifers before the weight can damage the branches and spoil the shape of the tree.*

PROTECT NEWLY PLANTED EVERGREENS

An evergreen planted in late summer or the autumn may not have grown new roots out into the soil, and if not watered regularly, it will not be able to absorb water as rapidly as it is lost. A windbreak for the first winter will reduce moisture loss and help a vulnerable plant to survive.

2 If you don't want to erect a shield, perhaps on aesthetic grounds, water in very dry spells to keep the roots moist, and cover the plant with a large plastic bag, pegged to the ground, when very severe weather is forecast. Remove it afterwards.

1 Insert three stout canes or stakes around the plant, then wrap a plastic sheet or several layers of horticultural fleece around the edge. Peg down the bottom.

PROTECT DELICATE ALPINES

Some alpines with hairy leaves are likely to rot if they become too wet and waterlogged during the cold months.

1 If you know that a particular alpine needs winter wet protection, cover it with a sheet of glass or rigid plastic substitute supported on special wires.

2 You can also use bricks to support and weight the pane. If you have a spare cloche, perhaps not needed until spring, you might be able to use this to protect alpines. Leave the ends open, but make sure that the cloche is firmly anchored and not likely to be lifted by strong winds.

SNOW PROTECTION

Conifers with an attractive or formal shape can be disfigured by a heavy fall of snow that pulls down or breaks the branches. If you live in an area of heavy snowfall, tie the branches, as shown. Green or brown twine is less conspicuous than string.

OVERWINTER TENDER FUCHSIAS

Most fuchsias are killed by frost, so unless you know that a particular variety is hardy enough to be left outdoors for the winter in your area, overwinter them in a frost-proof place.

1 If your fuchsias have been grown in pots during the summer, lift them to take into the greenhouse. If planted in the open soil, lift with a fork and remove excess soil.

2 Pot up the plants individually, or in large boxes if you have a lot of plants, then put them in a frost-free place, such as in the greenhouse or on a light windowsill indoors.

3 Tidy up the plants by removing old leaves and pinching out any soft green tips. You must keep the plants cool but frost-free, with the soil almost dry.

OVERWINTERING FUCHSIAS OUTDOORS

If you don't have a greenhouse or space indoors, try this method instead of throwing the plants away. Dig a trench about 30cm (12in) deep, line with straw, then lay the plants on this, as shown above. Cover the plants with more straw and then return the soil.

Dig them up in spring, pot them up and keep in warmth and good light to start into growth again. If the winters are not too harsh, many of the plants should survive.

PROTECTING HARDY FUCHSIAS

Hardy is a relative term, and although some fuchsias are tough enough for the roots not to be killed by frost where winters are not too severe, in cold areas they may succumb without a little extra protection.

Leave the old stems on, even though these will be killed, as this may afford the plant some additional shelter. To reduce the depth to which severe frosts penetrate, cover the crown with a thick layer of bracken, straw or peat, as shown here. Remove the protection in spring when the new shoots appear.

In mild areas, extra protection is not necessary for tough species such as *Fuchsia magellanica*.

OVERWINTER PELARGONIUMS

Pelargoniums, otherwise known as bedding geraniums, should be overwintered in a light and frost-free environment. If you have a lot of plants, a greenhouse is the best place to keep them, but if you do not have a greenhouse you may have space for a few plants indoors.

1 Lift the plants before the first frost if possible, though they will often survive a light frost if you take them in promptly afterwards.

2 Shake as much of the soil off the roots as possible, to reduce the size of the plant.

3 Trim the longest roots back to about 5–8cm (2–3in) long, to make potting up easier.

4 Shorten the shoots to about 10cm (4in), and trim off any remaining leaves. Although this looks drastic, new shoots will grow in spring, which you can use for cuttings if you want more plants.

5 The most effective way to store pelargoniums for the winter is in large trays at least 15cm (6in) deep. Half fill with soil or sowing compost (soil mix), position the plants and add more compost to cover the roots. Water well initially, then only when the soil becomes almost dry.

DEALING WITH YOUNG PLANTS

Fuchsias and pelargoniums can be rooted from cuttings taken in spring or autumn. If you are overwintering old plants, you can use them to provide plenty of cuttings in spring.

If you took cuttings in late summer or the autumn, however, your young plants will still be growing actively. Make sure that you keep these plants in good light and reasonably warm, in which case they will probably retain their foliage. If conditions are favourable, pelargoniums may even flower during the winter months.

6 If you want to overwinter your pelargoniums on a windowsill indoors, you may find it more convenient to use large pots instead of trays.

LATE AUTUMN

A LAST-MINUTE SPURT OF ACTION is often needed at this time of year, to get the garden ready for winter and to ensure protection for plants that need it. In cold areas winter will already have taken its grip, but in warmer climates there are still many mild days to be enjoyed. You should take advantage of them before colder temperatures and strong winds drive you indoors.

JOBS IN BRIEF

The Flower Garden

❑ Cut down the dead tops of herbaceous perennials
❑ Burn or compost garden refuse
❑ Remove pumps from the pond and store for the winter
❑ Plant roses
❑ Plant bare-root and balled trees and shrubs
❑ Clear summer bedding if not already done
❑ Finish planting spring bulbs as soon as possible
❑ Protect vulnerable plants that will remain in the garden
❑ Lift and take in chrysanthemums not hardy enough to overwinter outside
❑ Take hardwood shrub cuttings
❑ Collect and compost fallen leaves
❑ Remove leaves that have fallen on rock plants
❑ Cover alpines that need protection from winter wet with a pane of glass
❑ Protect the crowns of vulnerable herbaceous plants such as lupins and delphiniums from slugs by sprinkling coarse grit around them
❑ Remove pumps from ponds

TOP RIGHT: *Lifting chrysanthemum roots.*

BELOW LEFT: *Use a rooting hormone to help hardwood cuttings to root successfully.*

BELOW RIGHT: *Remove submersible pumps.*

The Greenhouse and Conservatory

❑ Clean and disinfect, ready for winter
❑ Check the minimum temperatures being achieved (if you don't have a minimum-maximum thermometer, buy one)
❑ Ventilate whenever the weather is mild enough
❑ Except with winter-flowering plants that are still in strong, active growth, gradually give plants less water. Most will then tolerate low temperatures better and disease should be less of a problem
❑ Check plants lifted for the winter

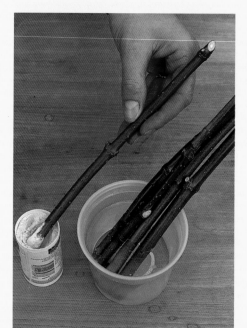

PLANTS AT THEIR BEST

Acer, colourful foliage (tree/shrub)
Berberis, colourful foliage and berries (shrub)
Cotoneaster, berries (shrub)
Fothergilla, colourful foliage (shrub)
Gentiana sino-ornata (alpine)
Liriope muscari (herbaceous)
Nerine bowdenii (bulb)
Pernettya, berries (shrub)
Pyracantha, berries (shrub)
Schizostylis coccinea (herbaceous)

LEFT: *Forthergillas are uninspiring for most of the year, with white flowers in late spring and early summer, but in autumn they take centre stage with brilliant leaf colouring.*

BELOW: Schizostylis coccinea *is always an eye-catcher in late autumn, when most other border plants have finished flowering.*

TAKE HARDWOOD CUTTINGS

Hardwood cuttings root more slowly than most of the softwood or semi-ripe cuttings that you can take during the spring and summer, but they need much less attention. They don't need heat, and because you plant them in the open ground (or in a cold frame), watering won't be an onerous chore.

Many shrubs, and even trees, can be raised from hardwood cuttings. Some of them are suggested in the box below.

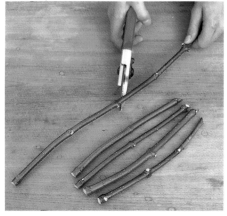

1 Choose stems that are firm and hard but not old and thick (pencil thickness is about right). With shrubs like this dogwood you should be able to make several cuttings from one shoot. The length of the cutting will depend on the plant, but about 15cm (6in) is appropriate for most. Make a cut straight across the stem, just below a node.

2 Make the second cut about 15cm (6in) above the first, and above a node, but this time at an angle so that you will know which is the top and which the bottom of the cutting.

3 Although a rooting hormone is not essential, it should increase the success rate, especially with plants that are difficult to root. Moisten the bases of the cuttings in water.

SHRUBS TO PROPAGATE

The list below is just a selection of the shrubs that usually root easily from hardwood cuttings, but there are many others. Be prepared to experiment, or consult a specialist book to see which plants are normally rooted by this method.
Aucuba japonica (spotted laurel)
Buddleia (butterfly bush)
Cornus alba (dogwood)
Cornus stolonifera (dogwood) – illustrated
Forsythia
Ligustrum ovalifolium (privet)
Philadelphus (mock orange)
Ribes sanguineum (flowering currant)
Roses (species and hybrids)
Salix (willow)
Spiraea
Viburnum (deciduous species)

4 Dip the moistened ends into a rooting powder. You can also use liquid and gel rooting hormones, in which case you should not dip the end in water first. Treat only the base end of each cutting.

5 Make a slit trench with a spade, a little shallower than the length of the cuttings. Choose a position where the cuttings can be left undisturbed for a year.

6 Sprinkle some grit or coarse sand in the base of the slit if the ground is poorly drained. This will help to prevent water-logging around the cuttings.

7 Insert the cuttings 8–10cm (3–4in) apart, upright against the back of the slit, leaving about 3–5cm (1–2in) above the ground.

8 Firm the soil around the cuttings, to eliminate the pockets of air that would cause the cutting to dry out.

9 Water the cuttings and label. Remember to water them in dry weather.

TREES FROM HARDWOOD CUTTINGS

Some trees can also be propagated from hardwood cuttings, and those below are particularly easy.

If propagating trees, decide whether you want a multi-stemmed tree or one with a single main stem. If the latter, set the cuttings deeper in the trench so that the top bud is just below the surface of the soil.

Platanus (plane)
Populus (poplar) – illustrated
Salix (willow)

LIFT AND PROTECT CHRYSANTHEMUMS

Not all autumn-flowering chrysanthemums have to be lifted (see box), but many do. The roots are potted into boxes, which means that you can start them off in warmth in spring.

1 Lift the roots after the plants have finished flowering and before severe frosts arrive.

2 Shake surplus soil off the roots before removing from the garden.

3 Trim the tops off and cut any long, straggly roots back to keep the root-ball compact.

4 Place a layer of soil or potting soil in a box or tray about 10cm (4in) deep. Position the roots and cover them with about 3cm (1in) of soil, firming lightly. Don't forget to label the plants. Keep the box in a cool, light place, such as a cool greenhouse, light garage windowsill, or a cold frame. For most types of chrysanthemum it does not matter if they receive a touch of frost. Keep the soil slightly damp but not wet.

BELOW: Chrysanthemum *'Countryman'*, is a reflexed early-flowering outdoor variety.

OVERWINTERING CHRYSANTHEMUMS

There are many kinds of chrysanthemum, but it is only the autumn-flowering chrysanthemums that are likely to cause confusion regarding overwintering.

In mild, frost-free climates they can all be left in the ground, and many of the species like *Chrysanthemum rubellum*, are hardy even in cold areas.

But in temperate climates the highly bred early-flowering autumn chrysanthemums are best lifted and stored, and even those outdoor ones that flower later are best treated this way. Even those that tolerate some frost are more likely to survive if kept fairly dry. Wet and cold is the combination to avoid.

PROTECT POND PUMPS

If you leave a pump in your pond over winter, ice may damage it. Don't just take it out of the pond and leave it where moisture can enter – store it in a dry place.

1 Remove submersible pumps from the water before penetrating frosts cause the water to freeze deeply.

2 Clean the pump before you put it away. It will probably be covered with algae which can be scrubbed off.

3 Remove the filter and either replace it or clean it. Follow the manufacturer's instructions.

4 Make sure all the water is drained from the pump. If your pump is an external one, make sure the system is drained.

DISPOSE OF YOUR RUBBISH . . . WISELY

Gardeners always acquire a lot of rubbish and debris in the autumn, but there is no one simple way to deal with it all. Be environmentally friendly and recycle as much as possible through composting.

To improve the chances of good compost, add a layer of manure or a proprietary compost activator after every 15cm (6in) of kitchen and garden refuse. Woody material such as hedge clippings and pruning will rot down too slowly to put straight on to the compost heap. These are best put through a shredder, then composted or used as a mulch. Some things are best burnt – diseased material and pernicious perennial weeds for instance, as well as woody material if you don't have a shredder. An incinerator that will burn the rubbish quickly is preferable to a traditional smoky bonfire.

A large quantity of leaves is better composted separately. Some leaves rot down slowly, but the end product is particularly useful for adding to potting mixtures.

5 Read the manufacturer's instructions, and carry out any other servicing that is necessary before storing the pump in a dry place. It may be necessary to send it away for a service, in which case do it now instead of waiting until spring.

WINTER

A well-planned garden will not be devoid of colour or interest in the winter months, and working outdoors can be a real pleasure. There are always jobs to be done, and tackling them now relieves the pressure in spring.
Sometimes there is no choice but to become an armchair gardener. This is the time to scan your gardening books and plant encyclopedias for ideas, perhaps plan minor improvements or even totally redesign your garden, and of course fill in your seed order – perhaps one of the most pleasurable jobs of all.

OPPOSITE: *Red-stemmed* Cornus alba *remain bright and interesting throughout the winter.*

ABOVE: *Focal points like this ornament can help to compensate for the lack of colour during the cold months.*

EARLY WINTER

THE ONSET OF WINTER INEVITABLY MEANS fewer jobs to do in the garden, but it is a good idea to get outdoors whenever the weather is favourable. There is always tidying-up to be done, and things like broken fences to be mended. It makes sense to get jobs like this finished before the more severe winter weather makes them even less appealing. This is an especially good time to take a critical look at how you can improve your soil in time for the next growing season.

JOBS IN BRIEF

The Flower Garden

❑ Check bulbs, corms and tubers in store
❑ Get rid of garden refuse by burning or composting
❑ Plant bare-root and balled trees and shrubs
❑ Check bulbs being grown in pots for early flowering
❑ Protect vulnerable plants
❑ Order seeds
❑ Service your mower
❑ Take hardwood shrub cuttings
❑ Take root cuttings
❑ Remove leaves from rockeries
❑ Protect alpines from winter wet with a pane of glass
❑ Protect flowers of winter plants vulnerable to the weather

The Greenhouse and Conservatory

❑ Once a week, check all plants and pick off any dead or dying leaves
❑ Ventilate on warm days
❑ Except with winter-flowering plants that are still in active growth, gradually give plants less water

TOP LEFT: *Service your lawn-mower and prepare it for winter storage.*

TOP RIGHT: *Protect low-growing winter-flowering plants with a cloche.*

RIGHT: *If you discover soft or diseased bulbs in store, dust the others with a fungicide.*

ABOVE: Jasminum nudiflorum, *one of the delights of winter.*

LEFT: Pyracantha *'Watereri', brilliant even in the grip of winter.*

PLANTS AT THEIR BEST

Chimonanthus praecox (shrub)
Erica carnea (shrub)
Erica × *darleyensis* (shrub)
Hamamelis mollis (shrub)
Iris unguicularis (syn. *I. stylosa*)
(herbaceous)
Ilex, berries (hollies)
Jasminum nudiflorum (wall shrub)
Liriope muscari (herbaceous)
Mahonia 'Charity' (shrub)
Nerine bowdenii (bulb)
Pernettya, berries (shrub)
Prunus × *subhirtella* 'Autumnalis'
(tree)
Pyracantha, berries (shrub)
Sarcococca (shrub)
Viburnum × *bobnantense* (shrub)
Viburnum farreri (syn. *V. fragrans*)
(shrub)
Viburnum tinus (shrub)

PROTECT WINTER HELLEBORE FLOWERS

Winter-flowering hellebores such as *Helleborus niger* (Christmas rose) are frost-hardy, but their pale blooms are often only just above soil level.

If you want to cut the flowers to take indoors, covering the plants will reduce mud splashes and keep the blooms clean and in good condition.

1 Protect low-growing winter-flowering plants such as *H. niger* with a cloche if you want perfect blooms to cut for indoors. Though frost-hardy, the flowers tend to become splashed with mud and damaged by the weather.

2 If you don't have a cloche, improvize with a piece of polythene (plastic) over wire hoops, or a pane of glass supported on bricks.

ABOVE RIGHT: Helleborus argutifolius *is a tall species that will not need protection.*

RIGHT: Helleborus orientalis *may benefit from protection for early cut blooms.*

CHECK BULBS AND CORMS IN STORE

Don't wait until it is time to plant your tender overwintering bulbs before checking them for rot. Storage rots are common, and easily spread from affected bulbs or corms to healthy ones.

1 Bulbs, corms and tubers being over-wintered in a frost-free place should be checked once a month. By eliminating diseased or soft bulbs or corms, you will prevent the rot spreading to others.

2 If you discover soft or diseased bulbs in store, it's worth dusting the others with a fungicide. Check with the label to ensure that it is suitable for the purpose, and be careful not to inhale the dust.

SERVICING YOUR MOWER

Winter is the best time to have your mower serviced. The chances are you won't bother once it is in regular use during the summer. You may prefer to have the servicing done professionally, which is often cheaper at this time than in spring, but you can do some of the simple tasks yourself. The advice below should be followed in conjunction with your handbook.

1 Remove accumulated clippings and dirt from around the blade housing of a rotary mower, being certain that any power supply is disconnected. Use an abrasive paper to clean metal blades.

2 Wipe the blade with an oily rag or spray with an anti-rust aerosol. If the blade is in poor condition, replace it with a new one. On appropriate models you may consider replacing it with a plastic blade for safety.

3 If you have a petrol (gasoline) mower, drain the fuel and oil before storing for the winter.

4 Remove the spark plug, clean it and reset the gap if necessary. If the plug is in poor condition, replace with a new one.

5 Pour a table-spoonful of oil into the cylinder and pull the starter to turn the engine over half a dozen times before you return the spark plug, thus coating the engine.

6 Brush or wipe away accumulated clippings from a cylinder mower. If the mower is electric, disconnect the power supply before you start.

7 Wipe the mower with an oily rag, or spray with an anti-rust aerosol, before you store it.

8 Oil the chain if your mower is fitted with one. You may have to remove the chain guard to reach it.

MID WINTER

IF YOU MADE AN EARLY START with winter jobs like digging and tidying beds and borders, mid winter is a time mainly for indoor jobs such as ordering seeds and plants, writing labels, and designing improvements for the year ahead.

These are not unimportant tasks, and by attending to them in good time, you are more likely to make the right decisions and have everything ready for late winter and early spring when gardening begins again in earnest.

JOBS IN BRIEF

The Flower Garden

- ❏ Check bulbs, corms and tubers in store
- ❏ Take root cuttings
- ❏ Take hardwood shrub cuttings
- ❏ Insulate cold frames for extra protection against the coldest weather
- ❏ Knock heavy snow off hedges
- ❏ Service your mower or have it done professionally

The Greenhouse and Conservatory

- ❏ Once a week check all plants and pick off any dead or dying leaves
- ❏ Ventilate on warm days
- ❏ Start off overwintered chrysanthemum stools (roots) to provide cuttings
- ❏ Start sowing seeds if you can provide sufficient warmth to germinate them and a very light position in which to grow the seedlings afterwards

TOP LEFT: *Chrysanthemum cuttings are easy to root, and now is a good time to take them.*

TOP RIGHT: *If a plant has large, fleshy roots, take cuttings close to the main stem.*

BELOW LEFT: *It is best to lift a young but well-established plant when taking root cuttings.*

BELOW RIGHT: *Start sowing summer flowers that need a long growing period before they flower.*

PLANTS AT THEIR BEST

Chimonanthus praecox (shrub)
Eranthis hyemalis (bulb)
Erica carnea (shrub)
Erica × darleyensis (shrub)
Galanthus nivalis (bulb)
Garrya elliptica (shrub)
Hamamelis mollis (shrub)
Iris unguicularis (syn. *I. stylosa*)
(herbaceous)
Ilex, berries (hollies)
Jasminum nudiflorum (wall shrub)
Lonicera fragrantissima (shrub)
Prunus × subhirtella 'Autumnalis'
(tree)
Sarcococca (shrub)
Viburnum × bodnantense (shrub)
Viburnum farreri (syn. *V. fragrans*)
(shrub)
Viburnum tinus (shrub)

LEFT: Garrya elliptica.

BELOW LEFT: Viburnum *x* bodnantense
'Dawn', in bloom in mid winter.

BELOW: Hamamelis mollis.

TAKE ROOT CUTTINGS

Nearly everyone takes stem cuttings at some time, but surprisingly few gardeners bother with root cuttings. Some useful plants can be propagated this way (see the box opposite for examples), and it is an interesting and relatively simple winter job, because root cuttings are only likely to be successful if taken during the dormant season.

1 Lift a young but well-established plant to provide the cuttings. If you don't want to use the whole plant for cuttings, and prefer to leave the parent plant largely undisturbed, just remove soil from one side to gain access to the roots.

2 If the plant has large, fleshy roots, cut some off close to the main stem or root. You should be able to make several cuttings from one root by cutting it into sections later.

3 Cut each root into lengths about 5cm (2in) long. To help you remember which way up they are, cut them horizontally at the top and diagonally at the bottom.

4 Fill a pot with a gritty potting mixture and insert the cuttings using a dibber or pencil to make the hole. The top of the cutting should be flush with the top of the potting soil.

5 Sprinkle a thin layer of grit over the surface. Label, as nothing will be visible for a few months, and it's easy to forget what the pot contains. Place in a cold frame or greenhouse and keep the potting soil just moist.

6 Some plants, such as border phlox and rock plants like *Primula denticulata*, have thin roots. These can be laid horizontally, so don't make sloping cuts to indicate the bottom. Just cut into 3–5cm (1–2in) lengths.

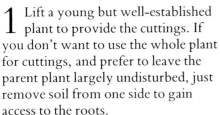

7 Fill a seed tray with a gritty compost (soil mix) and firm it level.

8 Space the cuttings out evenly over the surface, then cover them with a layer of the gritty potting mix. Keep moist but not too wet, in a cold frame or greenhouse.

SOME PLANTS TO GROW FROM ROOT CUTTINGS

Acanthus
Echinops
Gaillardia
Phlox (border)
Primula denticulata
Pulsatilla vulgaris
Romneya coulteri

LEFT: *Border phlox can be propagated from root cuttings. This one is* Phlox paniculata *'Flamingo'.*

INSULATE COLD FRAMES

Old-fashioned cold frames with brick or timber sides were not as light as modern aluminium and glass or plastic cold frames, but they were warmer. Glass sides let in more light, but also lose heat rapidly. Have the best of both worlds by insulating your glass-sided cold frame during the coldest weather, while taking full advantage of the glass sides in spring and summer.

1 Sometimes there are small gaps between the glass and an aluminium frame. This does not matter in hot weather, but for winter warmth it's worth sealing the gaps with draught-proofing strip sold for windows and doors.

2 Insulate the glass sides with sheets of expanded polystyrene (plastic foam). Cut with a knife or saw. Measure accurately, allowing for the thickness of the material where sheets join at the ends. Push sheets into place so that they fit tightly.

COVERING COLD FRAMES

Cold frames of any kind benefit from a warm blanket thrown over them on very cold nights. A piece of old carpet is an ideal alternative (see above). Put it in place *before* the temperature drops, and remember to remove it the next morning unless it remains exceptionally cold. Your plants need light and warmth.

TAKE CHRYSANTHEMUM CUTTINGS

Chrysanthemums that are overwintered in a greenhouse or cold frame are usually propagated from cuttings once the old stool (clump of roots) starts to produce shoots. It is better to raise vigorous young plants from cuttings than simply to replant the old clump. Chrysanthemums that have been boxed or potted up in the autumn, and kept frost-free and just moist, will soon start producing new shoots. Stimulate growth now with plenty of light and warmth.

1 When your boxes or pots of chrysanthemum stools have produced shoots about 5cm (2in) long, it is time to take cuttings.

2 If possible, choose shoots coming directly from the base of the plant. Cut them off close to the base.

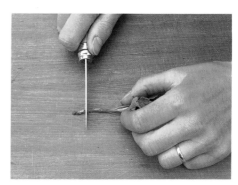

3 Pull off the lowest leaves and trim the ends of the cuttings straight across with a sharp knife.

4 Dip the ends in a rooting hormone. If using a powder, dip the end in water first so that it adheres. Hormone treatment usually improves the rate and speed of rooting.

5 Insert the cuttings around the edge of a pot containing a mixture suitable for cuttings.

6 If you don't have a propagator, cover the pot with a plastic bag, but inflate it to ensure it is not in contact with the leaves. Turn the bag regularly to avoid condensation dripping onto the leaves. Remove when the plants have rooted.

RIGHT: *Many chrysanthemums can make colourful garden plants for the autumn, and they are easily propagated from cuttings taken at this time of year.*

SOW SEEDS FOR SUMMER FLOWERS

It is too early to sow seeds outdoors, and it is likely to be too soon to sow most tender bedding plants in the greenhouse or on a windowsill. But it is not too soon to sow summer flowers that need a long growing period before they flower, such as fibrous rooted begonias (*Begonia semperflorens*). If in doubt, check the seed packet to see whether a particular flower needs early sowing or not.

Because it is difficult to provide the necessary warmth economically at this time of year, especially in a greenhouse, it is best to start the seeds off in a propagator, and move them out once they have germinated. By sowing in pots you will be able to germinate more kinds of seeds in your propagator at the same time. Sowing in pots is also sensible for seeds where only a few plants are needed, such as for trees and shrubs.

1 Fill the pot with a seed sowing compost (soil mix), and gently firm and level it. Using the base or top of a jar is a convenient way to do this.

2 Sow thinly, and as evenly as possible. Bear in mind that you have to handle the seedlings later, and very close spacing will make this difficult. Most can be sprinkled easily between finger and thumb, like salt.

3 Large seeds are best spaced individually. If they are very large, you can insert them into small holes made with a dibber.

4 Most seeds should be covered with a light sprinkling of the same soil mix. Use a sieve to spread the soil evenly. Some seeds germinate best in light and should not be covered – check the sowing instructions.

5 To avoid disturbing the evenly distributed seeds, water the pot initially by standing it in shallow water. Remove the pot and let it drain when the surface looks moist.

6 If you don't have a propagator, cover the pot with a sheet of glass or plastic until the seeds germinate. Turn the covering periodically if condensation is heavy. Don't forget the label!

LATE WINTER

IN FAVOURABLE AREAS LATE WINTER CAN be almost spring-like, especially in a mild winter, but don't be lulled into sowing and planting outdoors too soon. If the weather turns very cold, seeds won't germinate, and seedlings and plants may receive such a check to growth that they will not do as well as those sown or planted later. Concentrate your efforts on indoor sowing, but also make the most of cold frames and cloches in order to produce early crops in the kitchen garden.

JOBS IN BRIEF

The Flower Garden

- ❏ Plant climbers
- ❏ Feed and mulch beds and borders
- ❏ Order seeds, bulbs and plants for the coming season
- ❏ Insulate the cold frame for extra protection against the coldest weather
- ❏ Sow sweet peas
- ❏ Pinch out growing tips of autumn-sown sweet peas
- ❏ Tidy up the rock garden, and apply fresh stone chippings where necessary
- ❏ Check labels on shrubs and border plants, and renew if necessary
- ❏ Prune shrubs when the risk of frost is past

The Greenhouse and Conservatory

- ❏ Take chrysanthemum and dahlia cuttings
- ❏ Pot up chrysanthemums rooted earlier
- ❏ Sow seeds of bedding plants
- ❏ Prick out seedlings sown earlier
- ❏ Increase ventilation on warm days
- ❏ Ensure glass is clean so that the plants can receive plenty of light

TOP LEFT: *Sow seeds of bedding plants in a tray.*

TOP RIGHT: *Many summer bedding plants sown earlier will be ready to prick out.*

RIGHT *Take time now to tidy up the rock garden.*

PLANTS AT THEIR BEST

Crocus (bulb)
Daphne mezereum (shrub)
Eranthis hyemalis (bulb)
Erica carnea (shrub)
Erica × darleyensis (shrub)
Galanthus nivalis (bulb)
Garrya elliptica (shrub)
Helleborus niger (herbaceous)
Helleborus orientalis (herbaceous)
Iris unguicularis (syn. *I. stylosa*)
(herbaceous)
Iris reticulata (bulb)
Jasminum nudiflorum (wall shrub)
Muscari armeniacum (bulb)
Prunus cerasifera (tree)
Prunus × subhirtella 'Autumnalis'
(tree)
Sarcococca (shrub)
Viburnum × bodnantense (shrub)
Viburnum tinus (shrub)

RIGHT: *Varieties of* Erica carnea *flower in winter and often into spring.*

BELOW: *In mild areas,* Muscari armeniacum *will put in an appearance at the end of winter.*

TAKE DAHLIA CUTTINGS

If you require just one or two more dahlia plants, you can simply divide the tubers before planting them in late spring, making sure that each piece has an 'eye' or bud. For more plants, it is best to take cuttings after starting the tubers into growth early in the greenhouse.

1 Plant the tubers in deep boxes of compost (soil mix). You will not be able to bury the tubers, but trickle as much soil as possible around them. Keep the boxes in a light, warm place.

2 Take the cuttings when they have two or three pairs of leaves. If you take a tiny piece of the parent tuber, they should root quickly without a rooting hormone.

3 You can take larger cuttings if you miss the earlier stage, but try not to let them become longer than 8cm (3in). Cut off with a sharp knife just above the tuber.

4 Remove the lowest pair of leaves to leave a clear stem. Pull the leaves off carefully or cut them off with a sharp knife. If some of the leaves have grown large, cut these in half and discard the tips. This will reduce the area of leaf through which moisture can be lost while the cutting is rooting.

5 To increase the number of cuttings likely to root successfully, dip the cut ends into a rooting hormone. Insert the cuttings around the edge of a pot, label, then place in a propagator to root.

6 If you don't have a propagator, enclose the pot and cuttings in a plastic bag. Try to keep the leaves out of contact with the bag. They should root in a matter of weeks if you keep them in a warm, light position.

PLANT CLIMBERS

You can plant container-grown climbers at almost any time of the year provided the ground is not frozen or waterlogged. However, it is much easier to train in new shoots as they grow than it is to untangle them from their temporary support and attempt to retrain them.

1 Excavate a hole about twice the diameter of the root-ball. The centre of the plant should be at least 30cm (12in) away from the wall or fence, otherwise the roots will be too dry.

2 Dig in a generous amount of rotted manure or garden compost. This is particularly important when planting a climber near a wall or fence, as you need material that will hold moisture around the roots.

3 Tease out some of the fine roots from around the edge of the rootball, to encourage the plant to root out into the surrounding soil. Return and firm the soil around the plant, and apply a slow or controlled-release fertilizer.

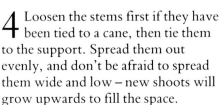

4 Loosen the stems first if they have been tied to a cane, then tie them to the support. Spread them out evenly, and don't be afraid to spread them wide and low – new shoots will grow upwards to fill the space.

5 Water thoroughly after planting, and be prepared to water regularly in dry weather for the first year. Climbers are usually planted where walls or other plants shield them from most of the rain.

6 Apply a mulch at least 5cm (2in) thick around the plant after the ground has been soaked thoroughly. This will reduce water loss as well as suppress weeds.

SOW BEDDING PLANTS

Late winter is a good time to sow the majority of frost-tender plants used for summer bedding if you have a heated greenhouse, although a few such as pelargonium (bedding geraniums) and *Begonia semperflorens* are best sown earlier to give them a long period of growth before planting out in late spring or early summer. Quick-growers, such as alyssum and French marigolds (*Tagetes* *patula*), will soon catch up even if you sow in early or mid spring.

Because you usually need quite a lot of each kind for bedding, it is normally best to sow the seeds in trays rather than pots. However, you may prefer to use pots for the more difficult seeds that need to be germinated in a propagator, as you can pack more in.

1 Fill a seed tray with a sterilized compost (soil mix) suitable for seeds and seedlings. A potting mix could inhibit germination or harm some seedlings. Strike the compost off level with the rim of the tray.

2 Use a presser board (a scrap of wood cut to the right size will usually do the job) and press the compost gently until it is firmed about 1cm (½in) below the rim.

3 Water the tray now, before you sow. This should provide enough moisture for the seeds initially, and won't wash fine seeds away or to one side of the tray.

4 Very large seeds can be spaced by hand, but most medium-sized seeds are easily scattered with a folded piece of stiff paper. Tap it with a finger as you move it over the surface.

5 Unless the packet advises not to cover the seeds (a few germinate better if exposed to light), cover them by sifting more of the sowing mixture over the top.

6 Unless you are placing the tray in a propagator, cover it with a sheet of glass, or place it in a plastic bag. Turn the glass over or the bag inside out regularly (it may be necessary to do this every day) to prevent condensation drips.

7 Remove any covering when the first seeds start to germinate. If you don't, the seedlings may succumb to diseases. It may be possible to reduce the amount of warmth needed once the seeds have germinated, but good light is essential.

SOWING FINE SEEDS

Very tiny seeds, like lobelia and begonia, are difficult to handle and to spread evenly. Mix them with a small quantity of silver sand to provide greater bulk, then sprinkle the sand and seed mix between finger and thumb as you move your hand over the surface of the tray.

PRICK OUT BEDDING PLANTS

Seeds sown in mid winter may be ready for pricking out, and even those sown in late winter may be ready to move on soon. Never let seedlings become overcrowded after germination.

1 Fill seed trays with a potting mixture recommended for seedlings. Strike the compost (soil mix) off level, then firm it with fingers or a pressing board.

2 Prick out a seedling by loosening the soil and lifting up the plant by its seed leaves (the first ones that open, which usually look very different from the proper leaves).

3 Make a hole in the potting mix, deep enough to take most of the roots without curling them. Gently firm the compost round the roots.

4 To help produce an evenly spaced box of plants, first prick out a row along the end and one side. When you have this spacing right, fill in the rest of the tray.

5 Exact spacing will depend on the type of plant you are pricking out. Large ones need more space than small ones. You are unlikely to fit more than 40 plants in a seed tray.

6 If you find it more convenient, use a modular tray system. This makes spacing easier, and there is less root disturbance when the plants are put in the garden later.

Suppliers

A selection of names has been given here for plants and garden accessories, but don't forget that the best place to start is often your local garden centre.

UNITED KINGDOM

GARDEN EQUIPMENT AND SUPPLIES
Atco-Qualcast Ltd.
Suffolk Works
Stowmarket
Suffolk IP14 1EY
Tel: 01449 612183
Lawnmowers, powered rakes and hedgetrimmers

Black and Decker Ltd.
Westpoint
The Grove
Slough SL1 1QQ
Tel: 01753 511234
Powered tools

Gardena UK Ltd.
Unit 7, Dunhams Court
Dunhams Lane
Letchworth
Hertfordshire SG6 1BD
Tel: 01462 686688
Watering systems, hand and powered tools

Sandvik Ltd.
Manor Way
Halesowen
West Midlands B62 8QZ
Tel: 0121 550 4700
Pruning tools

Two Wests & Elliott Ltd.
Unit 4, Carrwood Road
Sheepbridge Industrial Estate
Chesterfield
Derbyshire S41 9RH
Tel: 01246 451077
Greenhouse accessories and watering systems

Wolf Tools for Garden & Lawn Ltd.
Alton Road
Ross-on-Wye
Herefordshire HR9 5NE
Tel: 01989 767600
Garden and lawn tools

GARDEN NURSERIES
Bressingham Gardens
Bressingham, Diss
Norfolk IP22 2AB Tel: 01379 687464
Borderplants, alpines, trees and shrubs

Fryer's Nurseries Ltd.
Manchester Road
Knutsford
Cheshire WA16 0SX
Tel: 01565 755455
Roses, mainly hybrids

Notcutts Nurseries
Woodbridge
Suffolk IP12 4AF
Tel: 01394 383344

UNITED STATES

GARDEN EQUIPMENT AND SUPPLIES
Centre Landscaping and Supplies
Ross Highway
Alice Springs
NT 5750
Tel: (089) 52 4839

GARDEN NURSERIES
Arnhem Nursery
35 Arnhem Highway
Humpty Doo
NT 5791
Tel: (089) 88 1351

AUSTRALIA

GARDEN EQUIPMENT AND SUPPLIES
Centre Landscaping and Supplies
Ross Highway
Alice Springs
NT 5750
Tel: (089) 52 4839

The Happy Gardener
13 Aldous Place
Melville WA 6156
Tel: (09) 317 2520

Sherwyn
53-55 Canterbury Road
Montrose VIC 3765
Tel: (03) 728 9676

Australian Seed Company
5 Rosedale Avenue
Hazelbrook
NSW 2779
Tel: (047) 58 6132

GARDEN NURSERIES
Arnhem Nursery
35 Arnhem Highway
Humpty Doo
NT 5791
Tel: (089) 88 1351

Perrots Nursery
Deception Bay Road
Deception Bay
QLD 4508
Tel: (07) 888 3737

Yarralumla Nursery
Banks Street
Yarralumla
ACT 2600
Tel: (06) 207 2444

NEW ZEALAND

GARDEN EQUIPMENT AND SUPPLIES
California Green World
Garden Centre
139 Park Road
Miramar
Wellington
Tel: (04) 388 3260

Palmers Garden World
Cr. Shore &
Orakei Roads
Remuera
Auckland
Tel: (09) 524 4038

GARDEN NURSERIES
Big Trees
Main Road
Coatesville
Auckland
Tel: (09) 415 9983

Kent's Nurseries
Cr. Fergusson Drive
& Ranfurly Street
Trentham
Tel: (4) 528 3889

Index

Page numbers in *italics* refer to illustrations.

ACKNOWLEDGMENTS

Key: t = top; b = bottom; c = centre; l = left; r = right.

All specially commissioned photography taken by Peter Anderson except for the following:
Paul Forrester: pages 17tr; 81bl, cb, br.
Jacqui Hurst: page 63t.

ADDITIONAL PICTURE CREDITS
The publishers would like to thank the following picture libraries for granting their permission to
reproduce the images in the book.

Jerry Harpur: 7 t (Exbury Gardens Hants), c, b; 8 (designer, Susan Whittington); 9;
11 tl; 29 l (Barnsley House, Gloucs), r; 32 (Fudlers Hall, Mashbury); 33
(Anne Alexander-Sinclair); 35 l & br (Park Farm, Chelmsford) tr; 43 t (Marcus Harpur), b (Park Farm, Chelmsford); 47 t
(Albert Williams), b (Sticky Wicket); 52 (The Dingle, Welshpool); 53; 57 t (Penny Crawshaw); 71 b (designer Beth Chatto);
76 (designer, Beth Chatto); 77 (designers, Brian Daly and Allan Charman);
79; 83 bl br.

Peter McHoy; 11 tr, b; 18 br; 20 br; 27 br; 31 tr; 37 br; 38 bl; 39 tl, ct, tr, bl, cb; 44 bl; 48 br; 51 br; 55 b;
58 bl; 59 br; 61 cl, cr, bl, br; 63 bl, br; 65 b, cl; 66 tl, ct, tr, br; 67 bl; 71 t; 72 bl; 73 br; 80 tr, c;
83 t; 85 c; 86 br; 89 b.